The
WISDOM of POOH

Timeless Insights for Success & Happiness

Dr. Simon Crawford Welch
& Michael Finn, RRP, CGP

CONTENTS

ABOUT THE AUTHORS

Dr. Simon Crawford Welch

Simon Crawford Welch, PhD, brings a unique blend of personal experience, academic insight, and a lifelong passion for storytelling to his work as an author. In his latest endeavor, *The Wisdom of Pooh: Timeless Insights for Success & Happiness*, Simon draws on the beloved world of the Hundred Acre Wood to offer readers profound insights into personal growth, resilience, and the value of simplicity. His approach to writing and leadership is deeply influenced by his diverse life experiences and a career that spans continents and industries, making his perspective both globally informed and universally relatable.

A self-described global nomad, Simon's journey began in Ethiopia and Djibouti, where he spent his early years immersed in diverse cultures that shaped his understanding of people and the world around him. His education in the UK, followed by leadership roles across North America and Mexico, added layers of experience that continue to influence his writing. With a career that includes executive leadership positions in hospitality and digital marketing, Simon's professional path has been anything but conventional. He has learned firsthand the importance of perseverance, adaptability, and the courage to embrace change—qualities that resonate with the lessons embedded in A.A. Milne's beloved tales of Winnie the Pooh and his friends.

Throughout his career, Simon has been recognized as a visionary leader, steering organizations toward growth and transformation. As the former President & Chief Operating Officer of Diamond Resorts International, he led the company through significant expansion, managing a network of 160 resorts across 14 countries. His time in Mexico as President of Tesoro Resorts and Chief Sales & Marketing Officer of Royal Resorts further deepened his understanding of cultural dynamics and the art of connecting with people from all walks of life. These leadership experiences have informed his approach to writing, where he aims to distill complex ideas into accessible, meaningful insights.

Simon's life and work have always been guided by a philosophy that values the simplicity and clarity found in the stories of the Hundred Acre Wood. In *The Wisdom of Pooh: Timeless Insights for Success & Happiness*, he uses the adventures of Pooh, Piglet, Tigger, and Eeyore as a lens through which to explore enduring themes such as empathy, resilience, and the power of kindness. He believes that the lessons found in Pooh's world—whether it's the art of doing nothing, the importance of friendship, or the courage to step out of your comfort zone—offer valuable guidance for navigating today's complex and fast-paced world.

The book reflects not only Simon's professional expertise but also his personal journey of growth and reinvention. Having lived in or visited over 100 countries, he brings a worldly perspective to his writing, drawing on a lifetime of learning from different cultures and experiences. His global outlook allows him to see the connections between the simple wisdom of Winnie the Pooh and the challenges of modern life, making his interpretations of Milne's stories both timeless and timely.

Simon's personal experiences have also deeply shaped his understanding of the themes explored in the book. Facing financial setbacks, coping with personal loss, and raising a child with special needs have taught him the true meaning of resilience and the value of *The Wisdom of Pooh's* simple joys. These lessons find their way into his writing, where he weaves together the whimsical world of the Hundred Acre Wood with practical advice for leading a more meaningful life. He encourages readers to find strength in simplicity, to embrace their own unique paths, and to discover the profound wisdom that can often be found in the quiet moments.

Simon is not just an author; he is a lifelong learner and teacher, dedicated to helping others find clarity and purpose in their own lives. His work at The Critical Thought Lab, an organization committed to fostering critical thinking and personal development, further reflects his belief in the power of reflection, simplicity, and authentic connection. In *The Wisdom of Pooh: Timeless Insights for Success & Happiness*, he offers readers more than just an exploration of Milne's classic tales; he provides a guide to living a more intentional, compassionate, and fulfilling life.

Through his writing, Simon Crawford Welch invites us all to return to the simple wisdom of Pooh and his friends—to slow down, listen more, and approach life with an open heart. Whether you're a leader seeking inspiration, a parent navigating the challenges of daily life, or simply someone looking for a bit of comfort and guidance, *The Wisdom of Pooh: Timeless Insights for Success & Happiness,* offers timeless advice for embracing the journey with grace, humility, and a touch of honey-sweet joy.

Simon is the author of numerous articles and papers, two other books: "American Chasms: Essays on the Divided States of America," "Forever Young: A Father's Guide to the Rocky Road of Life," and co-author of "Marketing in Hospitality and Tourism: A Consumer Focus."

Michael Finn, RRP, CGP

Michael is a seasoned leader, award-winning innovator, and published author with over 25 years of experience in sales, marketing, and executive management across various industries. His unique blend of expertise, ranging from hospitality and vacation ownership to experiential marketing and brand development, brings a fresh and practical perspective to his writing, including his latest co-authored work, *The Wisdom of Pooh: Timeless Insights for Success & Happiness* .

Throughout his career, Michael has demonstrated a talent for transforming challenges into opportunities and achieving remarkable growth. His leadership journey has taken him from serving as Vice President at Revolve Marketing to National Director roles at Marriott Vacations Worldwide and Diamond Resorts International. At Marriott, he was instrumental in expanding experiential marketing programs by 100% annually over three years, driving more than $60 million in referral revenue and over $30 million in experiential sales. This success was achieved through innovative strategies that engaged customers and created lasting brand loyalty.

Currently, Michael serves as Chief Development Officer at The BluWater Group and President of Conexus, LTD, where he leads a team of experts specializing in sales efficiency, marketing, and operational excellence. His hands-on approach and passion for driving results have earned him a reputation for being a dynamic leader who understands the intricacies of various sales environments, from call centers to on-the-ground marketing locations.

In *The Wisdom of Pooh: Timeless Insights for Success & Happiness*, Michael draws from his extensive experience to explore the simple yet profound wisdom found in A.A. Milne's beloved stories. By connecting the timeless adventures of Pooh and his friends to practical insights on leadership, growth, and resilience, he offers readers a guide to navigating the complexities of modern life with a touch of whimsy and grace.

Beyond his professional achievements, Michael is dedicated to continuous learning and personal development, with training in Six Sigma, leadership techniques, and brand synergy. His writing reflects not only his business acumen but also his belief in the power of kindness, connection, and lifelong learning—values that resonate deeply with the spirit of the Hundred Acre Wood.

Whether developing marketing strategies, leading high-performance teams, or sharing the gentle wisdom of Winnie the Pooh, Michael brings a unique blend of experience, creativity, and heart to everything he does.

ACKNOWLEDGEMENTS

Dr. Simon Crawford Welch

This book is, at its heart, a labor of love, born from a deep desire to pass on timeless wisdom and gentle guidance to someone very dear to me—my son, Greyson Beckett Maloney Welch. Greyson, you are the light that inspires every page, every word, and every lesson in this book. As I wrote, I imagined you exploring the world, facing its trials and tribulations with the same boundless curiosity and quiet strength that Winnie the Pooh and his friends show in the Hundred Acre Wood. My hope is that these simple stories and the wisdom they carry will help you find your way, especially during times when life feels confusing or overwhelming. May you always know that, just like Pooh and Piglet, you are never alone. There is always love, laughter, and support waiting for you, wherever you go.

To my partner, Jamie—you are the rock upon which this project was built. Your endless patience and the creative energy you poured into designing and formatting this book have made it come alive in ways I could have only dreamed. You took my words and ideas and transformed them into something beautiful, adding your own touch of magic to every chapter. There were late nights and countless revisions, yet you met each moment with grace and encouragement, believing in this project even when I had my doubts. This book would not be the same without you, and I am forever grateful for your dedication, your eye for detail, and most of all, your love.

To my co-author, Michael Finn, thank you for tolerating my idiosyncrasies. You were the turbo-charge needed to get this book out of my head and onto paper. I am forever grateful.

To A.A. Milne and the timeless world of the Hundred Acre Wood—you have given the world stories that are so much more than just tales for children. They are a source of comfort and a beacon of wisdom for readers of all ages. I am humbled to contribute to the legacy of these beloved characters, and I hope that my reflections will help others see the depth and warmth hidden in each of Pooh's simple, gentle words.

And finally, to anyone who picks up this book—thank you for taking this journey with me. I hope that as you turn each page, you are reminded of the power of kindness, the beauty of simplicity, and the magic of simply being present. If this book offers even a moment of comfort, a bit of insight, or a feeling of connection, then it has served its purpose.

May you all find your own Hundred Acre Wood—a place of refuge, reflection, and quiet joy—no matter where life takes you. And Greyson, always remember: life's adventures may not always be easy, but with a little bit of love, a dash of courage, and a friend by your side, you can overcome anything.

Michael Finn

First and foremost, I would like to extend my deepest thanks to my friend, Simon, for inviting me to join this remarkable venture. This book was his brainchild, and I was thrilled to be brought on board to offer additional perspectives. While my previous writing has often focused on business initiatives, which has been gratifying in its own way, this project has brought a new kind of joy. It's a unique experience to explore life lessons through the timeless wisdom of Winnie the Pooh and his friends—characters who have been inspiring us since A.A. Milne first published these stories nearly a century ago, in 1926. Thank you, Simon, for this opportunity.

The beauty of this book lies in the freedom it gave me to draw upon my own life, recalling memories and experiences shared with friends and family. Each chapter allowed me to reflect on real-life moments, while also thinking about how these lessons might resonate with my children. It's a delightful parallel to the way A.A. Milne crafted the original stories for his son, Christopher Robin Milne—a gesture of such devotion and inspiration.

In this spirit, I'd like to thank my parents and siblings for providing me with an upbringing that allowed me to appreciate these stories deeply and, ultimately, expand upon them. As always, my gratitude goes to my wife, Camilla, and my children, Michaela and William, who inspire me every day to put my thoughts into words. I'm also deeply grateful to my friends, colleagues, and mentors for guiding me along a path as enriching and vibrant as the Hundred Acre Wood.

Thank you all.

FOREWORD

In an era where leadership is often associated with grand strategies, complex solutions, and cutting-edge innovations, there is a growing realization that the timeless principles of simplicity, empathy, and resilience may hold the true key to effective leadership. The fast-paced demands of modern life and business can leave us feeling overwhelmed and disconnected from what really matters. It is in this context that *The Wisdom of Pooh: Timeless Insights for Success & Happiness* offers a refreshing and insightful perspective, drawn not from the latest management fads but from the gentle wisdom of a beloved childhood character—Winnie the Pooh.

The idea that a bear of very little brain, as Pooh humbly refers to himself, could offer meaningful lessons in leadership might seem counterintuitive at first glance. However, as the chapters of this book unfold, it becomes clear that the very simplicity with which Pooh approaches life is precisely what makes his wisdom so profound. In *The Wisdom of Pooh*, we are invited to journey through the Hundred Acre Wood and discover how the simple joys, friendships, and life lessons found there can be applied to the challenges of our own lives, both personally and professionally.

Embracing Simplicity in a Complicated World

The core message we offer throughout this book is the value of simplicity—an increasingly rare and often overlooked trait in today's leadership culture. We live in a world that tends to celebrate complexity, where the answers to problems are often buried in layers of jargon, analysis, and ever-evolving theories. Yet, as we demonstrate, true leadership lies not in over complicating matters but in distilling them to their essence. Pooh's quest for honey is a metaphor for any leader's pursuit of success; it's not about devising the most elaborate strategy but about staying focused on what is truly important, being persistent, and enjoying the journey along the way.

We do not suggest that simplicity is synonymous with a lack of ambition or a disregard for depth. Rather, it shows how a simple approach to leadership allows for greater clarity and effectiveness. When leaders simplify, they can communicate more clearly, act more decisively, and inspire more authentically. Pooh's adventures illustrate how embracing simplicity can lead to more meaningful connections and more joyful living—principles that resonate deeply in the realm of leadership.

The Power of Connection

Winnie the Pooh is not a solitary figure; his experiences are interwoven with those of his friends—Piglet, Tigger, Eeyore, and others. Each of these characters brings a different perspective, teaching us about the importance of empathy, understanding, and connection. In the business world, these relationships mirror the dynamics within teams and organizations. Leaders who cultivate genuine relationships, like Pooh does, foster a sense of belonging and trust that no amount of technical skill or business acumen can replace.

The Wisdom of Pooh emphasizes that true leadership extends beyond mere transactional interactions. It is about building a culture where people feel valued, heard, and appreciated. The lessons drawn from Pooh's interactions with his friends show that when leaders prioritize the well-being of their teams, the results are not just better productivity but deeper loyalty and more meaningful collaboration. In this way, the book reminds us that the heart of leadership is not only about guiding others but also about connecting with them on a human level.

Resilience, Adaptability, and Bouncing Back

An additional theme that runs throughout The Wisdom of Pooh is resilience—the ability to recover from setbacks and adapt to changing circumstances. The inhabitants of the Hundred Acre Wood face challenges that, while seemingly small in scale, teach valuable lessons in resilience and problem-solving. Whether it's Eeyore dealing with a lost tail or Tigger finding his place in the world, each character's experiences provide practical insights into overcoming adversity and embracing change.

Leaders today face an unprecedented rate of change and unpredictability. The Wisdom of Pooh offers not just theoretical concepts but actionable advice on how to maintain a positive outlook, stay grounded, and continue moving forward despite obstacles. Drawing from the steadfastness of Pooh and the energy of Tigger, readers will learn how to turn setbacks into opportunities for growth, finding the silver lining in every situation.

Wisdom That Transcends Age and Time

The teachings of Winnie the Pooh are not bound by age or profession; they resonate as powerfully with adults navigating corporate corridors as they do with children exploring the magical world of the Hundred Acre Wood. This book bridges the gap between the childlike wonder of Pooh's adventures and the practical demands of adult life. It provides a framework for applying the seemingly simple philosophies of Pooh and his friends to the complex world of leadership.

What sets *The Wisdom of Pooh* apart from other leadership books is its ability to blend practical strategies with whimsical storytelling. Each theme weaves together leadership principles with anecdotes from the beloved tales, offering readers a lighthearted yet deeply impactful approach to self-improvement. It encourages leaders to find joy in the mundane, to appreciate the journey rather than just the destination, and to remember that sometimes, the best course of action is simply to "do nothing" and reflect.

A Guide to Living and Leading with Purpose

At its heart, *The Wisdom of Pooh* is a guide to living and leading with purpose. It encourages us to slow down, to pay attention to the simple joys that we often overlook in our hurry to achieve the next big goal. By revisiting the lessons of Pooh and his friends, we are reminded that wisdom does not always come from formal education or complex theories. Sometimes, the most profound truths are found in the most unassuming places—such as a bear's quiet wisdom about life, love, and honey.

As you embark on this journey through the quotes and stories of *The Wisdom of Pooh*, we encourage you to approach each lesson with an open heart and a spirit of curiosity. Let the stories and insights guide you toward a leadership style that is not only effective but also enriching for yourself and those around you. Ask yourself, "What would Winnie do?" when faced with challenges, and you may find that the answers are simpler, kinder, and more profound than you had ever imagined.

This book is more than just a collection of self-development advice; it is a call to rediscover the simplicity, joy, and wisdom that reside within each of us. Whether you are a seasoned executive or just starting your leadership journey, there is something timeless and universal in Pooh's gentle approach to life that can help you navigate the complexities of the modern world with grace and success.

So, take a moment to pause, breathe, and embrace the lessons of the Hundred Acre Wood. Let *The Wisdom of Pooh* be your guide to simplifying, connecting, and succeeding in every aspect of your life.

Simon & Michael

November 2024

PERSONAL GROWTH AND SELF-IMPROVEMENT

Now comes the fun part: how can we use the wisdom of Winnie the Pooh and his friends in real-life situations? Can Winnie the Pooh answer questions that we've been asking for ages? We believe the answer is a big YES! With his calm and thoughtful approach, Pooh shows us how to simplify complicated problems, relax, and enjoy life's journey, giving us a bit of an advantage over others.

The first step in using these lessons is figuring out what happiness, growth and success mean to you. Everyone sees these things a little differently. For many, happiness, growth and success come from family and love; for others, it's about moving up in their career and gaining power. Some find it in solitude and inner peace. One thing noticeably missing from this list is money. Money is just a tool; it helps you reach your goals. But if you end up with a billion dollars and never enjoyed your life or felt the love of family and friends, is that really success?

Success, growth and happiness are personal and can look different for everyone. Pooh and his friends offer us various perspectives on what it means to live a fulfilled life. Pooh's constant search for honey is a simple but powerful symbol of following your passions. Piglet's courage, despite being small, teaches us about bravery and conquering self-doubt. Tigger's enthusiasm shows us the strength of positivity and energy. And even Eeyore, with his gloominess, reminds us how important it is to recognize our feelings and stay resilient.

One of the biggest lessons from Winnie the Pooh is the power of simplicity. In a world that can feel overwhelming, Pooh's knack for finding joy in simple things inspires us to clear the clutter from our lives, both physically and mentally. By focusing on what really matters, we can lower stress and improve our well-being. Simplifying life doesn't mean avoiding responsibilities, but rather prioritizing our actions and thoughts to match our values and goals.

Winnie the Pooh teaches us to enjoy the journey, not just the end goal. Life is made up of many moments, and finding joy in the present can change our daily experiences. Whether it's a quiet time with a friend, the satisfaction of solving a problem, or simply enjoying a favorite snack, these little pleasures come together to create a meaningful life. Pooh's adventures in the Hundred Acre Wood remind us to cherish these moments, helping us feel content and grateful.

The characters in the Hundred Acre Wood show us that there is no single definition of success. For Rabbit, success might mean having a well-kept garden; for Owl, it could be seeking knowledge; and for Kanga, it's about her child's well-being. These different viewpoints encourage us to think about our own definitions of success and to chase goals that are truly important to us, rather than those set by society. In our quest for success, it's important to remember that material wealth isn't the ultimate goal. Money can help us enjoy experiences and provide comfort, but it's our relationships, personal growth, and the impact we have on others that truly define a successful life. Pooh's world, free from material excess, reminds us that wealth can take many forms, friendships, adventures, and moments of true happiness.

As we explore the quotes, stories, and lessons from Winnie the Pooh and his friends, let's embrace the wisdom they share. By using these lessons in our lives, we can make our approach to challenges simpler, appreciate the journey, and redefine success in ways that bring us real fulfillment and joy. Join us as we discover these timeless teachings, finding guidance and inspiration in the gentle wisdom of the Hundred Acre Wood.

As you read through the upcoming chapters, filled with quotes from Pooh and his friends, we encourage you to find the ones that speak to you the most. Think about these quotes and the lessons they offer. Decide what your next step will be in using this wisdom in your own life. Whether it's simplifying a complicated situation, enjoying the present moment, or redefining what success means to you, let the gentle guidance from the Hundred Acre Wood light your way.

THE POWER OF NETWORKING

"A day without a friend is like a pot without a single drop of honey left inside."

Winnie the Pooh

One morning in the Hundred Acre Wood, Winnie the Pooh found himself staring at an empty honey pot. It was one of those quiet, lonely moments that made him realize something was missing—not just honey, but the company of friends. Pooh thought to himself, *"A day without a friend is like a pot without honey."* Determined not to let the day go to waste, he set off to visit Piglet, hoping for some company (and maybe a little honey). As the day unfolded, Pooh's visits to Piglet, Eeyore, and Rabbit transformed what could have been a dull, lonely day into one filled with laughter, stories, and shared moments. By the end of the day, Pooh felt fulfilled—not because he had found more honey, but because he had reconnected with his friends.

This story captures the essence of networking: much like Pooh's search for honey and friendship, networking is about proactively seeking out relationships, not waiting for them to come to you. Whether in personal life or business, meaningful connections don't just happen by chance—they are built through effort, engagement, and mutual support. Pooh's journey reminds us that relationships, like honey, are sweeter when shared. In the professional world, the same applies: taking the time to connect with others can turn a solitary venture into a network of support, opportunities, and growth. Networking is about more than just making contacts—it's about cultivating the kind of relationships that, like Pooh's friendships, bring joy and lasting value.

Creating Your Own Opportunities

Pooh's adventure offers a valuable lesson that resonates beyond the boundaries of the Hundred Acre Wood. Many people wait for opportunities to come to them, hoping that luck or circumstance will bring success. However, real progress often comes from stepping out of your comfort zone, taking initiative, and being proactive in pursuing what you want. Pooh teaches us that sometimes, we must create our own opportunities rather than waiting for them to find us.

There's the old saying that you cannot wait for your ship to come in... you have to swim out to it. Look at Sara Blakely's story as a great example of the power of networking. Sara is the founder of Spanx. Before she became a billionaire entrepreneur, she was selling fax machines door-to-door. She had an idea for a new kind of undergarment but didn't wait for someone to discover her or recognize her talent. Instead, she took matters into her own hands. Sara designed a prototype, pitched her concept to manufacturers—most of whom initially rejected her—and kept refining her approach until she found a company that believed in her vision. Her persistence paid off, and her willingness to step out and create her own opportunity led to the creation of a multi-billion-dollar company. Blakely's story serves as a powerful example of how taking action can transform an idea into reality, even when the path is filled with obstacles.

Another compelling example is J.K. Rowling, who was famously rejected by 12 different publishers before *Harry Potter* found a home and became a global phenomenon. Instead of giving up, she kept submitting her manuscript and continued writing, believing in her story and her ability to make it successful. Her persistence and networking paid off in a big way, turning her into one of the most celebrated authors in the world.

Like Pooh leaving his corner of the Forest, neither Blakely nor Rowling sat back and waited for recognition; they went out and pursued it, turning rejection into motivation.

The Importance of Networking

Networking is an essential element in creating your own opportunities and driving personal and professional growth. Just as Winnie the Pooh ventured out to visit his friends in the Hundred Acre Wood, we too must take the initiative to connect with others in our fields, communities, and social circles. Networking is more than simply meeting people and exchanging business cards; it's about forming genuine relationships built on trust, mutual interest, and shared goals. These connections can open doors to new possibilities, spark collaborations, and propel growth in ways that sheer luck or individual talent alone cannot.

Opportunities often arise through people rather than by chance. While having a good idea or strong skills is important, connecting with the right individuals can amplify your efforts and create pathways that you wouldn't have discovered on your own. Being proactive, reaching out, and making a conscious effort to build relationships increases your chances of finding new avenues for success. Whether you're a budding entrepreneur, an established professional, or even a student, networking can be the bridge that connects you to your next opportunity.

The Power of Building Authentic Relationships.

At its core, networking is about cultivating authentic relationships that are based on genuine interest and value, rather than just transactional exchanges. Forming real connections with others goes beyond trying to "get something" from someone. It's about building a network where each person feels heard, appreciated, and valued. When you invest in the relationships you form, you're not just collecting contacts; you're building a support system that can offer advice, resources, introductions, and encouragement.

For example, think about how Steve Jobs and Steve Wozniak, co-founders of Apple, first met. It wasn't in a boardroom or through a business networking event. Jobs and Wozniak were introduced by a mutual friend who knew they shared an interest in electronics. What started as a friendship and a mutual hobby eventually turned into one of the most successful business partnerships in history. The initial bond was built on shared passion and curiosity, and from that authentic connection grew a groundbreaking technology company.

Reid Hoffman, the co-founder of LinkedIn, is another prime example of the power of networking. Before launching the professional networking platform, Hoffman spent years building connections in Silicon Valley, where he formed relationships with other entrepreneurs, investors, and tech influencers. He understood that success in the tech industry wasn't solely about having a groundbreaking idea; it was also about surrounding himself with people who could help turn that idea into reality. Hoffman's ability to nurture these relationships and leverage his network played a significant role in the successful launch and growth of LinkedIn, which went on to become the world's largest professional network. By building a web of meaningful connections, he was able to secure resources, advice, and support that ultimately fueled the platform's growth.

Networking Beyond the Corporate World.

While networking is often associated with career advancement or business growth, its benefits extend far beyond the professional sphere. It can also play a vital role in personal development, community engagement, and even creative pursuits. The relationships you build can offer valuable life advice, emotional support, and new perspectives that contribute to your personal growth.

Look at Maya Angelou's story, the renowned poet and author. Throughout her career, Angelou built a powerful network of friends and mentors who helped shape her work and provided guidance during difficult times. Her close relationships with prominent figures such as Oprah Winfrey, James Baldwin, and Malcolm X played a significant role in her life and work. These relationships were built on mutual respect, shared values, and a deep commitment to social justice. Angelou's network of friends and colleagues not only enriched her life but also helped amplify her voice, enabling her to inspire millions around the world.

In the world of arts and entertainment, the story of The Beatles is another great example. Before becoming one of the most influential bands in history, The Beatles struggled to find success in Liverpool. They built a network of musicians, club owners, and promoters who believed in their talent and helped them get gigs. Their connections with other musicians, such as Rory Storm and the Hurricanes (Ringo Starr's original band), helped solidify their lineup and improve their sound. These early networking efforts played a crucial role in getting the band noticed and eventually signing a record deal. The relationships they formed along the way were instrumental in their journey to stardom.

The Ripple Effect: How One Connection Can Change Everything.

The beauty of networking is that even a single connection can have a ripple effect, leading to numerous other opportunities. When you meet someone new and form a meaningful connection, you're not just connecting with that one person—you're potentially opening the door to their entire network. This means that one genuine relationship can expand into many more, creating a web of connections that may lead to new partnerships, job offers, or even friendships.

Take, for instance, the example of Howard Schultz, the former CEO of Starbucks. Schultz initially worked in sales and marketing at a small kitchen appliance company when he noticed that one of his clients, a small coffee shop chain called Starbucks, was purchasing a large number of coffee makers. Intrigued, he reached out to the company's founders and formed a relationship with them. This connection ultimately led him to join Starbucks and eventually transform it from a small local coffee retailer into a global coffeehouse empire. Schultz's story illustrates how a single networking opportunity can alter the course of a career and lead to groundbreaking success.

Overcoming Networking Anxiety

It's not uncommon to feel like Eeyore at a social event, standing in the corner and unsure of how to start a conversation. Networking can feel intimidating, especially if you're naturally introverted or new to the scene. However, just as Pooh took the initiative to visit his friends in the Hundred Acre Wood, you can take small steps to make networking more approachable and less daunting.

- **Start Small**. Instead of trying to meet everyone at a large event, set a goal to have meaningful conversations with just a few people. Quality is more important than quantity when it comes to building genuine relationships.

- **Seek Common Ground**. Much like Pooh's friends found joy in the simple things they shared, look for common interests to break the ice. This could be a shared profession, hobby, or even a mutual connection.

- **Be Authentic**. Don't approach networking with the mindset of *"What can this person do for me?"* Instead, think about how you can add value to their lives or careers. Genuine interest and curiosity can set the foundation for a meaningful relationship.

- **Practice Active Listening**. Pay close attention to what the other person is saying. Ask follow-up questions and show that you're truly engaged in the conversation. People appreciate being heard, and this can help strengthen the connection.

Networking in the Digital Age

In today's world, networking isn't limited to face-to-face interactions. Social media platforms like LinkedIn, Twitter, and even Facebook offer valuable tools for building professional connections. However, the same principles apply—authenticity, value, and relationship-building.

Look at Gary Vaynerchuk, probably the most prominent social media influencer and entrepreneur there is. Vaynerchuk started by networking online, engaging with people on social media, offering valuable advice, and providing free content that helped others succeed. His authentic and consistent online presence allowed him to build a network of millions of followers, many of whom became clients, collaborators, or partners. Gary's approach to online networking wasn't just about promoting himself; it was about engaging meaningfully with his audience, answering questions, and genuinely trying to help others succeed. As a result, his network became a powerful asset in building his business ventures.

Practical Steps to Build a Strong Network.

To truly harness the power of networking, it's important to take intentional steps toward building and maintaining relationships. Here are some actionable tips to help you get started:

- **Follow Up**. After meeting someone, whether at an event or online, make a point to follow up. A simple email or LinkedIn message saying, *"It was great to meet you"* can go a long way. Keeping in touch helps solidify the connection and keeps you on the other person's radar.

- **Give Before You Receive**. Offer your help, share valuable information, or introduce someone to a contact who could be useful to them. By giving first, you build goodwill, and people are more likely to reciprocate in the future.

- **Stay in Touch**. Don't just reach out when you need something. Keep your relationships warm by occasionally checking in, sharing articles that might interest them, or simply catching up over coffee.

- **Leverage Online Platforms**. Use LinkedIn to connect with industry professionals, join relevant groups, and participate in discussions. Share content that reflects your interests and expertise to engage your network.

- **Attend Industry Events**. Conferences, meetups, and workshops are great places to meet like-minded individuals. Attend these events regularly and make it a point to introduce yourself to at least a few new people each time.

- **Develop a Networking Mindset**. See every interaction as an opportunity to build a relationship. Whether you're at a social gathering, work function, or online, approach networking with an open mind and a genuine interest in others.

The Takeaway: Networking as a Lifelong Skill.

Networking is not just something you do when you're looking for a job or launching a business—it's a lifelong skill that can enhance your personal and professional growth. Much like Pooh in the Hundred Acre Wood, you must be willing to step out of your corner, explore new connections, and nurture the relationships you form. Remember, networking isn't about instant results; it's about planting seeds and cultivating those relationships over time.

The relationships you build today could lead to opportunities you never expected in the future. Just as a single conversation could transform a career, one new connection could lead to a life-changing partnership or a lifelong friendship. So go ahead, take that step, and start building your network. The Hundred Acre Wood may be a fictional place, but the lessons from Pooh and his friends about the value of connection are very real and can guide you in creating your own opportunities in the vast forest of life.

THE POWER OF SELF-BELIEF

"You're braver than you believe, stronger than you seem, and smarter than you think."

Christopher Robin

One sunny afternoon in the Hundred Acre Wood, Christopher Robin found Winnie the Pooh sitting quietly under a tree, looking a little sad. Worried, Christopher Robin walked over to his friend.

"Why so sad, Pooh?" he asked.

Pooh sighed. "I was just thinking about all the things I can't do. I'm not very brave, I'm not very strong, and I'm certainly not very smart."

Christopher Robin knelt down and looked Pooh in the eye. "Pooh, you're braver than you believe, stronger than you seem, and smarter than you think."

Pooh tilted his head, thinking about those words. Christopher Robin's reassurance filled him with new confidence. Maybe he wasn't giving himself enough credit.

The Importance of Believing in Oneself

Christopher Robin's words remind us how important it is to believe in ourselves. Self-belief is the foundation of confidence, which is key to achieving success in both personal and professional life. When we believe in ourselves, we're more likely to take risks, face challenges, and go after our goals with determination and strength.

Many people struggle with something called 'Imposter Syndrome.' This is when someone feels anxious or doubts their success, even though they are doing well and achieving a lot. It often makes people feel like they're a 'fraud' or not good enough, even when their abilities say otherwise.

Imposter Syndrome can affect anyone from college students to CEOs. People from all walks of life, even those who are smart, driven, creative, and successful, often have trouble recognizing their own accomplishments. It's especially common in competitive workplaces, where performance is always being measured and competition is encouraged. Many successful leaders experience imposter syndrome. Unfortunately, it's still often seen as a taboo topic or a sign of weakness, when in fact, that's not true at all. It's a common issue that doesn't get the attention it deserves.

Imposter syndrome affects even the men and women we see as the most confident and successful. It's estimated that 70% of women and 50% of men will face imposter syndrome at some point in their careers. In today's workplace, it's like a shadow that follows many of us.

Sometimes, we just need to remember that no matter how much self-doubt we feel, the people around us, even our biggest role models, are probably dealing with it too.

Don't believe us? Read on.....

"The high regard people have for my work makes me very uncomfortable. I feel like I've tricked them without meaning to."

— Albert Einstein

"You think, 'Why would anyone want to see me in another movie? And I don't even know how to act, so why am I doing this?'"
— Meryl Streep, Actor

"I still believe that any day now, the no-talent police will come and arrest me."
— Mike Myers, Actor, Comedian, Producer

"Even after selling 70 million albums, I was still thinking, 'I'm no good at this."
— Jennifer Lopez, Entertainer

"I've written 11 books, but every time I think, 'Uh oh, they're going to find out. I've fooled everyone, and they'll catch me.'"
— Maya Angelou, Author, Poet, and Civil Rights Activist

"Every time I was called on in class, I was sure I was about to embarrass myself. Every time I took a test, I thought I did poorly. And every time I didn't embarrass myself — or even did well — I believed I had fooled everyone again. One day, I thought, they'd figure it out... This feeling of capable people being filled with self-doubt has a name — imposter syndrome. Both men and women experience it, but women tend to feel it more strongly and let it hold them back."
— Sheryl Sandberg, former COO of Facebook

"The funny thing about imposter syndrome is you bounce between extreme confidence and complete panic, like: 'I'm a fraud! Oh no, they've figured me out!'... Just try to enjoy the confidence when it comes, and ride out the feeling of being a fraud."
— Tina Fey, Comedian

"I am not a writer. I've been fooling myself and others."
— John Steinbeck, Author

"The biggest challenge for me has been the voice in my head, which I call my 'obnoxious roommate.' I wish someone would invent a tape recorder to capture everything we say to ourselves. We'd see how important it is to stop that negative self-talk. It's about pushing back against that voice with a bit of wisdom."
— Arianna Huffington, Author & Editor

"I still sometimes feel like the awkward kid in high school. Every morning, I have to remind myself that I'm a superstar so I can get through the day and be what my fans need me to be."
— Lady Gaga, Grammy and Academy Award Winner

"Since my time at Princeton, through law school and in my career, I've never quite felt like I fully belonged. I'm always looking over my shoulder, wondering if I measure up."
— Sonia Sotomayor, First Hispanic Supreme Court Justice

"When I get recognized for my acting, I feel really uncomfortable. I tend to retreat inward. I feel like a fraud, and any moment, someone's going to find out I don't deserve any of what I've achieved."
— Emma Watson, Award-winning Actress, Model, and Activist

"It was the same when I first walked onto Yale's campus. I thought everyone would realize the mistake and take back the Oscar. I imagined someone knocking on my door

saying, 'Sorry, that was meant for Meryl Streep.'"
Jodie Foster, Academy Award-winning Actress

"There are many people out there who think I'm an expert. How do they believe all this about me? I know so many things I don't know."
Dr. Margaret Chan, ranked by Forbes as the thirtieth most powerful woman in the world in 2013

"I still feel a bit of impostor syndrome... That feeling doesn't go away that you shouldn't take me too seriously. What do I know? I share this with you because we all have doubts about our abilities, our power, and what that power really is."
— Michelle Obama

Imposter syndrome is more than just feeling like a fraud; it shows up in many different ways. It might appear as insecurity, self-doubt, fear of failure, or perfectionism. It can also come as self-criticism, low self-esteem, an inability to accept compliments, or a focus on where you're falling short. It happens when there's a clash between how you see yourself and what you believe others expect from you. Or it can be a clash between the standards you set for yourself and how you judge your performance.

At the heart of imposter syndrome is the fear of not being good enough. This feeling might not always be there, but when it shows up, you seriously doubt yourself and your abilities and feel very insecure. You worry that you'll say the wrong thing or be exposed. You feel comfortable with your ideas when they're just in your head, but as soon as you speak them, you worry they will be judged. You imagine that everyone will turn and focus their attention on you. It thrives on fear, and when you're afraid, it's much harder to remember everything you've learned so far. When you feel anxious, you experience it both mentally and physically. Your mind races, and the fight-or-flight response kicks in. When you see how common this feeling is, you might start to notice—if only for a moment—that there's something else happening here... And maybe, just maybe, your self-assessment isn't accurate... Perhaps you are not an imposter at all.

The Research

Research consistently shows that self-confidence is a key factor in success. A study published in the Journal of Personality and Social Psychology found that self-confidence is more important for achieving success than talent. The study revealed that people with high self-confidence were more likely to set challenging goals, keep going when faced with obstacles, and ultimately reach their ambitions.

Another study by the National Bureau of Economic Research found that people with higher self-confidence tend to earn more money. This research highlighted that self-confident individuals are more likely to seek out opportunities, negotiate well, and show leadership qualities that help them advance in their careers. Specifically, the study showed that self-confidence can lead to a 3% increase in wages over a lifetime, emphasizing the financial benefits of believing in oneself.

Techniques to Build Self-Belief and Self-Confidence

Building self-belief and self-confidence is a journey that takes practice and commitment. Here are some proven techniques to help you develop these important qualities:

- **Positive Affirmations.** Positive affirmations are powerful tools for building self-belief. By repeating positive statements about yourself, you can train your brain to have a more positive self-image. For example, saying, *"I am capable and confident"* can help strengthen your belief in your abilities. A study published in Social Cognitive and Affective Neuroscience found that positive affirmations activate the brain's reward centers, which boosts self-esteem and confidence. Participants who practiced positive affirmations showed greater resilience to stress and performed better in challenging tasks.

- **Visualization.** Visualization means imagining yourself reaching your goals. This technique builds self-confidence by creating a clear image of success. Athletes often use visualization to boost their performance, and it can be just as helpful in other areas of life. Research by Dr. Shelley Taylor at UCLA showed that visualization can improve performance and raise self-confidence. Participants who pictured themselves successfully completing a task were more likely to reach their goals than those who didn't use visualization.

- **Set Achievable Goals.** Setting and achieving small, realistic goals can boost your self-confidence. Each small success strengthens your belief in your ability to reach bigger goals. Start with tasks that are easy to manage and gradually take on more challenging ones as your confidence increases. A study in the *Journal of Applied Psychology* found that setting goals greatly improves self-efficacy and performance. Participants who set specific, challenging goals saw bigger improvements in self-confidence and task performance compared to those with vague or simple goals.

- **Practice Self-Compassion.** Self-compassion means being kind and understanding to yourself, especially in tough times. It helps boost self-confidence by lowering self-criticism and promoting a positive view of yourself. Dr. Kristin Neff's research on self-compassion shows its benefits for mental health and self-confidence. Her studies reveal that people who practice self-compassion have less anxiety and depression, along with higher self-esteem and resilience.

- **Seek Feedback and Learn.** Constructive feedback can be very helpful for building self-confidence. Seek feedback from trusted mentors, colleagues, or friends, and use it to improve your skills and performance. Embrace a

THE POWER OF SELF-BELIEF   25

growth mindset by seeing challenges as chances to learn and grow. A study published in the Harvard Business Review found that people who actively sought feedback and used it to improve themselves showed significant increases in self-confidence and performance. Feedback helps highlight areas for growth and strengthens your sense of progress and achievement.

- **Celebrate Your Successes.** Take time to celebrate your achievements, no matter how small. Recognizing your successes strengthens your belief in your abilities and encourages you to keep pursuing your goals. Research by Teresa Amabile at Harvard Business School highlights the importance of celebrating small wins. Her study found that acknowledging progress and celebrating successes boosts motivation, productivity, and overall self-confidence.

Winnie the Pooh and his friends remind us that believing in ourselves is vital for reaching our goals and living a fulfilling life. Christopher Robin's words show us that we are capable of more than we think. By building self-belief and self-confidence, we can overcome challenges, achieve our dreams, and inspire others to do the same. So, take these lessons to heart and remember that you are braver, stronger, and smarter than you realize. Embrace your potential and let your self-belief guide you to success.

EMBRACING YOUR TRUE SELF

"The things that make you different are the things that make you, you."

Winnie the Pooh

In Hundred Acre Wood, each character brings something special to their little community. Winnie the Pooh is always searching for honey, Tigger is known for his energetic bouncing, and Eeyore often adds a touch of sadness. But it's Piglet, with his small size and big heart, who shows us the power of individuality.

One day, the residents of the Hundred Acre Wood decided to hold a grand parade to celebrate friendship. Each character was given a role. While everyone was excited, Piglet felt anxious. He worried that his small size and quiet nature couldn't contribute much to such a big event. Sensing his friend's unease, Pooh gently reminded Piglet, *"The things that make you different are the things that make you, you."*

Encouraged by Pooh's words, Piglet set out to create something special. He made intricate, delicate decorations that only someone of his size and patience could manage. On the day of the parade, Piglet's contributions added a unique charm, showing that his individuality was not a burden but a gift.

Piglet's experience teaches us an important lesson: our differences are our strengths. In real life, we often feel pressured to fit in and hide our unique traits. However, as Piglet showed, embracing what makes us special can lead to amazing contributions.

Authentic Leadership: What It Is and What It Isn't

Authentic leaders are rare, and their honesty sets them apart. It's important to understand what authentic leadership is not:

- Compromising your values to get ahead.

- Taking credit for someone else's work.

- Saying only what others want to hear.

- Pretending to be someone you're not.

- Hiding your flaws and weaknesses.

- Making decisions based on politics.

- Valuing popularity over principles.

- Blaming others for your mistakes.

In contrast, authentic leadership involves:

- Making decisions based on your values.

- Living your principles with integrity.

- Always giving credit where it's due.

- Showing empathy and compassion.

- Recognizing and admitting your flaws.

- Owning your mistakes and fixing them.

- Doing what's right, even when it's hard.

- Holding yourself and others accountable.

When you lead with authenticity, you build a culture of trust, engagement, high performance, and psychological safety. Your team will follow you not because they have to, but because they want to.

The Importance of Authenticity in Relationships

Authenticity is not only important for leadership; it's also essential for building real relationships. Studies have shown that being authentic in relationships leads to greater emotional intelligence (EI) and emotional quotient (EQ). Research published in the Journal of Social and Personal Relationships found that people who are authentic are more likely to form deeper, more meaningful connections with others. They tend to be more empathetic, trustworthy, and effective communicators.

Authenticity builds trust, which is the foundation of any strong relationship. When we are true to ourselves, we show others that we are reliable and sincere. This encourages them to respond in kind, creating a cycle of trust and openness.

Research and Statistics on Authenticity

Dr. Brené Brown, a research professor at the University of Houston, has studied the power of vulnerability and authenticity extensively. In her book *"The Gifts of Imperfection,"* she writes, *"Authenticity is a collection of choices we have to make every day. It's about the choice to show up and be real. The choice to be honest. The choice to let our true selves be seen."* Her research shows that people who embrace vulnerability and authenticity are happier, more resilient, and feel a stronger sense of belonging. She highlights that embracing authenticity requires courage—the courage to be imperfect, to set boundaries, and to be vulnerable. She indicates that people who practice authenticity are more likely to build meaningful connections, as they create environments where others feel safe to share and be themselves. This openness leads to stronger relationships both personally and professionally.

An additional study published in the Journal of Counseling Psychology supports Brown's findings. Researchers found that people who score high on measures of authenticity report greater life satisfaction and well-being. These individuals tend to have strong self-awareness, understanding their strengths and weaknesses, and are comfortable expressing their true selves. This self-awareness is linked to lower levels of anxiety and depression because authentic individuals are less likely to feel pressured to conform to external expectations. Moreover, authentic individuals are more likely to engage in fulfilling relationships. They attract others who value honesty and integrity, leading to deeper and more meaningful connections. The study also found that authentic people tend to have higher self-esteem and better mental health overall. They are resilient in the face of challenges because their self-worth comes from within, not from external approval.

Research in the Harvard Business Review highlights the impact of authenticity in leadership. Authentic leaders—those who are genuine, open, and ethical—create an environment of trust and loyalty among their teams. Employees working under authentic leaders report higher job satisfaction, greater engagement, and better performance. This link between authentic leadership and positive workplace outcomes shows the importance of authenticity beyond personal relationships, extending its benefits into professional settings.

In yet another study, the Gallup organization found that employees who see their leaders as authentic are more likely to stay with their companies longer. This loyalty comes from the trust and respect that authentic leaders build, making employees feel valued and understood. Authentic leadership also encourages a culture of openness and psychological safety, where team members feel comfortable sharing ideas and taking risks without fear of judgment.

The bottom line is that there is a large body of research that highlights the significant benefits of authenticity. Embracing authenticity not only enhances personal happiness and resilience but also strengthens relationships and improves professional outcomes. By choosing to be real, honest, and vulnerable, we can create environments that foster trust, engagement, and overall well-being.

Applying the Lesson to Your Life

Embracing your individuality is about recognizing, valuing, and leveraging what makes you unique. The story of Piglet teaches us that our perceived limitations can often be our greatest strengths. By understanding this lesson, we can approach life with greater confidence and authenticity, paving the way for deeper personal fulfillment, stronger relationships, and professional success. Here's how you can actively apply these principles in your own life:

- **Recognize and Celebrate Your Unique Traits.** The first step in embracing your individuality is to recognize the qualities that set you apart. Think about the traits, experiences, and perspectives that make you who you are. Reflect on what you've been through, your interests, your strengths, and even your perceived weaknesses. These elements come together to form your personal story, which is unlike anyone else's.

- ◦ **Self-Reflection Exercise**. Take some time to list your unique traits. What do you do differently from others? What have you achieved that others may not have? What struggles have you overcome? This can help you identify qualities that make you special.

- ◦ **Reframe Your Perceived Weaknesses**. If there's a trait you've always seen as a limitation, ask yourself how it might actually be a strength. For instance, Piglet's small size was initially viewed as a drawback, but it became an asset when he needed to slip into tight spaces or approach situations with a gentler touch. If you're introverted, for example, recognize that this quality can make you an excellent listener or someone who is thoughtful and detail-oriented.

- **Practice Authenticity in Your Daily Interactions.** Living authentically means expressing yourself honestly and being true to your values, even when it feels uncomfortable. Authenticity is not just about saying what you feel; it's about aligning your actions with your beliefs. When you practice authenticity, you invite others to know the real you and form deeper, more meaningful connections.

  - ◦ **Be Honest About Your Thoughts and Feelings**. In conversations, share your opinions, even if they differ from those of others. You don't have to be confrontational, but expressing your perspective adds value and encourages diverse thinking. Remember, innovation often comes from those who think differently.

  - ◦ **Align Your Actions with Your Values**. If you value kindness, for example, make it a point to practice acts of kindness every day. If you value honesty, strive to be transparent in your communication, even when it's challenging.

  - ◦ **Set Boundaries**. Being authentic also means setting boundaries. Learn to say no to things that do not align with your values or goals. It's okay to prioritize your needs over others' expectations. When you honor your boundaries, you show respect for yourself, which in turn earns the respect of others.

- **Surround Yourself with Supportive People.** Your environment plays a significant role in shaping your ability to live authentically. Make sure to surround yourself with people who appreciate and support the real you. Authentic relationships are built on mutual respect and understanding, and they encourage you to be yourself.

  - ◦ **Evaluate Your Social Circle**. Reflect on whether your current relationships are supportive and positive. Are there people in your life who encourage you to be your authentic self? Are there relationships that drain your energy or make you feel like you have to hide parts of who you are? Consider reducing time spent with people who don't support your growth.

- **Seek Out Like-Minded Communities**. Join groups, clubs, or online forums where you can meet people with similar interests or values. Being part of a community where you feel accepted can give you the courage to be yourself in other areas of your life.

- **Encourage Authenticity in Others**. By showing support for others' true selves, you create an environment where authenticity is valued. Celebrate your friends' and colleagues' unique qualities, and encourage them to pursue their passions.

- **Leverage Your Individuality in Professional Settings.** In the workplace, people often feel pressure to conform or present themselves in a certain way. However, your unique perspective can be a powerful asset in your career. Innovation, creativity, and growth often stem from diverse viewpoints and ideas.

  - **Share Your Perspective**. Don't be afraid to contribute ideas that differ from the mainstream. Often, the most groundbreaking solutions come from those who think outside the box. For example, if you approach problems from an unconventional angle, you might offer a solution that others wouldn't have considered.

  - **Embrace Your Unique Work Style**. You might have a different approach to getting things done, and that's okay. If you're someone who prefers to work independently or think deeply before sharing ideas, let that be part of your process. Adapt your work environment to fit your needs as much as possible, whether that means scheduling time for focused work, taking breaks to refresh your mind, or seeking out collaborative projects that align with your interests.

  - **Develop Your Personal Brand**. Think about what makes you unique in your industry or profession. What do you bring to the table that others may not? This could be a specific skill set, a unique way of thinking, or a particular passion. Use this to build your personal brand and distinguish yourself from others.

- **Embrace Lifelong Growth and Learning.** Part of being authentic is accepting that you are a work in progress. This means continuously striving to grow, learn, and evolve. Authenticity is not about being rigid in who you are; it's about being honest about where you are on your journey and open to learning along the way.

  - **Adopt a Growth Mindset**. View challenges as opportunities to learn rather than obstacles to success. Understand that mistakes and failures are part of the process. A growth mindset encourages you to embrace new experiences and learn from them.

- **Regularly Reflect on Your Progress**. Set aside time to assess whether you're living in alignment with your values. Are there areas where you could be more authentic? Are there situations where you felt pressured to conform, and how can you navigate them differently next time?

- **Stay Curious**. Keep exploring your interests, hobbies, and passions. Your individuality will naturally evolve as you grow, and that's a good thing. The more you learn and experience, the more you add depth to your authentic self.

- **Draw Strength from Role Models Who Embraced Their Individuality.** There are countless examples of people who embraced their individuality and, in doing so, made a significant impact on the world. Learning from their stories can inspire you to be true to yourself and take pride in your uniqueness.

- **Albert Einstein**. He once said, *"The person who follows the crowd will usually go no further than the crowd. The person who walks alone is likely to find themselves in places no one has ever been before."* He was considered eccentric and unconventional, but his unique way of thinking led to some of the greatest scientific breakthroughs in history. Einstein's story reminds us that thinking differently can be a strength, not a weakness.

- **Malala Yousafzai**. The youngest Nobel Prize laureate, she remained true to her values of education and equality despite facing extreme adversity. Her courage to stand up for what she believed in has inspired millions worldwide. By embracing her authenticity, she not only changed her own life but also impacted the lives of countless others.

- **Steve Job**s. Co-founder of Apple, he was known for his visionary approach and commitment to his unique design philosophy. He didn't conform to the traditional way of doing things; instead, he embraced his individuality and focused on creating products that combined technology with artistry. His ability to stay true to his vision revolutionized multiple industries.

- **Use Your Individuality to Make a Positive Impact.** Embracing your authentic self isn't just about personal gain; it's also about contributing to the world in a way that only you can. Your unique perspective, skills, and experiences can bring fresh insights, inspire others, and drive positive change.

- **Identify Causes or Issues You're Passionate About**. Leverage your talents and experiences to contribute to a cause that matters to you. Whether it's volunteering, advocating for social change, or creating art that inspires, using your unique traits to make a difference can be incredibly fulfilling.

- **Mentor Others**. Share your journey with people who are struggling to embrace their individuality. Your story could be exactly what someone else needs to hear. By guiding others to accept themselves, you not only reinforce your own authenticity but also create a supportive community.

- **Innovate Through Your Unique Lens**. If you have a particular skill or passion, find ways to use it to solve problems or create something new. For example, if you're a creative thinker, consider how you can apply that creativity to address an issue in your field or community.

Embracing Your Authentic Path

Piglet's story teaches us that our differences are not flaws but unique attributes that add value to our lives and the lives of others. When we embrace our individuality, we give ourselves permission to live authentically, pursue our passions, and make meaningful contributions. By recognizing and celebrating what makes us unique, practicing authenticity, surrounding ourselves with supportive people, leveraging our strengths in our careers, and committing to lifelong growth, we not only pave the way for our own success but also inspire those around us to do the same.

Remember that embracing your individuality is not a one-time decision; it is an ongoing journey of self-discovery and self-expression. It requires courage, but as you live more authentically, you'll find that the rewards—personal fulfillment, stronger relationships, and meaningful impact—are well worth the effort. In doing so, you'll not only step out of your own corner but will also encourage others to do the same, contributing to a world where everyone's unique voice is valued and celebrated.

LEAVING THE CORNER OF THE FOREST

"You can't stay in your corner of the Forest waiting for others to come to you. You have to go to them sometimes."

Winnie the Pooh

Winnie the Pooh's wise words remind us of the importance of stepping out of our comfort zones to grow and connect with the world. Pooh and his friends often go on new adventures, sometimes reluctantly. One day, Pooh realized he was running low on honey and needed to leave his cozy corner to visit Rabbit and ask for some. Pooh loved his comfortable spot, but his need for honey pushed him to venture out, leading to delightful conversations and a new understanding of the world beyond his usual surroundings. This simple story illustrates a powerful truth: growth and new experiences come from stepping outside our familiar places. Pooh's willingness to leave his corner of the Forest not only helped him get honey but also strengthened his friendships and broadened his experiences.

Understanding the Comfort Zone

A comfort zone is a mental, emotional, and behavioral state where we feel safe, relaxed, and in control. It consists of familiar routines, predictable activities, and situations where we experience low levels of stress and anxiety. In this zone, life is comfortable and secure because we know what to expect, and our abilities match the challenges we face. While staying in the comfort zone provides a sense of stability and relief from stress, it can also act as a barrier that prevents us from growing, learning, and achieving our full potential.

To truly thrive, it is important to understand the balance between the Comfort Zone and the Growth Zone. Each serves a purpose, but they offer very different outcomes.

The Characteristics of the Comfort Zone

The comfort zone is appealing because it feels secure and predictable. Here are some characteristics of this state:

- **Safety and Familiarity.** The comfort zone consists of tasks, activities, and behaviors that are familiar to us. There is little risk involved, which means we are less likely to face failure, disappointment, or rejection. This is the space where we perform tasks on autopilot without having to think too much or exert extra effort.

- **Minimal Stress.** There is a low level of anxiety in the comfort zone because the challenges are minimal or manageable. We don't need to stretch our abilities or step out of our boundaries. While this may feel good in the short term, it often leads to stagnation over time.

- **Routine.** Life within the comfort zone is characterized by routine and repetition. We follow the same patterns every day, which gives us a sense of stability. While routines can be helpful for managing daily life, they can also limit our ability to experience new things and grow as individuals.

- **Short-Term Satisfaction.** The comfort zone offers immediate gratification and relief from stress, making it an easy place to stay. It provides short-term satisfaction without pushing us toward long-term fulfillment or growth.

While there is nothing inherently wrong with being in the comfort zone—especially when we need a break or some time to recharge—staying there for too long can keep us from realizing our potential and discovering what we are truly capable of.

The Characteristics of the Growth Zone

The Growth Zone, on the other hand, requires us to step out of our comfort zone and into a place where we encounter new experiences, face challenges, and learn new skills. Here are some defining characteristics of the growth zone:

- **New Challenges.** In the growth zone, we engage in activities and tasks that push us beyond our current limits. These challenges may feel intimidating at first, but they also provide opportunities for development. Stepping into this zone forces us to confront our fears, doubts, and insecurities.

- **Learning and Adaptation.** The growth zone is where learning happens. When we take on new challenges, we gain new knowledge and acquire skills that we didn't have before. We learn to adapt to different situations, environments, and circumstances. This helps us build resilience and develop problem-solving skills.

- **Increased Confidence.** Each time we overcome a challenge or achieve a goal outside of our comfort zone, our confidence grows. We realize that we are more capable than we initially thought. This increased self-belief makes it easier to tackle future challenges and step into even bigger growth opportunities.

- **Expanded Opportunities.** By consistently stepping into the growth zone, we open ourselves up to new possibilities and experiences that would not be accessible if we stayed within the boundaries of our comfort zone. New connections, career opportunities, and personal development milestones often arise when we embrace the unknown.

- **Long-Term Fulfillment.** While the comfort zone offers short-term relief, the growth zone provides long-term satisfaction. The sense of accomplishment that comes from overcoming obstacles and achieving meaningful goals leads to a deeper sense of fulfillment.

The Comfort Zone vs. The Growth Zone: Why Both Matter

It's important to recognize that both the comfort zone and the growth zone have their place. The comfort zone isn't inherently negative. In fact, it serves a crucial function by providing a space where we can rest, recharge, and reflect. Sometimes, it's necessary to retreat to the comfort zone for stability and to regain energy before taking on new challenges. However, if we remain in the comfort zone for too long, it becomes a place of stagnation where growth is limited, and we may start to feel unfulfilled or complacent.

The growth zone, on the other hand, can be challenging and even uncomfortable. It requires us to face uncertainties, take risks, and make mistakes. However, it is also where we discover our true potential. The more time we spend in the growth zone, the more we grow, and the more confident and resilient we become. To truly live a fulfilling life, we need to find a balance between the two zones—resting in the comfort zone when needed but consistently pushing ourselves into the growth zone to evolve and achieve more.

Expanding the Boundaries of Your Comfort Zone

The beauty of the growth zone is that each time we step into it, we push the boundaries of our comfort zone a little further. What once felt challenging or intimidating eventually becomes routine, and the cycle continues as we seek out new growth opportunities. For instance, if you fear public speaking, the thought of giving a presentation might feel daunting. But once you face that fear and give a presentation, public speaking starts to feel less intimidating. The growth zone eventually becomes part of your expanded comfort zone.

Practical Strategies to Move from the Comfort Zone to the Growth Zone

- **Set Small, Achievable Goals.** Start by setting small, manageable goals that stretch you just a little outside of your comfort zone. This could be something as simple as trying a new hobby, introducing yourself to someone new, or learning a new skill. Each small step helps you build momentum and prepares you for bigger challenges.

- **Embrace Failure as a Learning Opportunity.** When stepping into the growth zone, it's important to understand that mistakes and failures are part of the process. Rather than viewing setbacks as signs of inadequacy, see them as valuable learning experiences. Ask yourself, *"What can I learn from this?"* and use the insights to improve.

- **Use the "10% Rule".** The "10% Rule" suggests pushing yourself to do something that is just 10% more challenging than what you are currently comfortable with. This makes growth feel less overwhelming and more achievable. For example, if you're used to running 2 miles, try running 2.2 miles the next time. If you're comfortable with giving a presentation to 10 people, aim for an audience of 11 or 12.

- **Surround Yourself with Growth-Oriented People.** The people you surround yourself with can have a significant impact on your mindset and motivation. Seek out individuals who encourage you to challenge yourself, take risks, and grow. Their support and shared experiences can inspire you to embrace new opportunities.

- **Visualize Your Success.** Before stepping into the growth zone, take a moment to visualize what success will look and feel like. Imagine yourself overcoming the challenge and experiencing the rewards. This mental preparation can increase your confidence and motivation.

- **Reflect on Past Achievements.** Think about times when you stepped out of your comfort zone in the past and succeeded. Remind yourself of the progress you've made and the resilience you've developed. This reflection can help boost your confidence and encourage you to keep pushing forward.

Real-World Examples of Stepping Out of the Comfort Zone

- **Elon Musk's Bold Ventures.** Elon Musk is well-known for his ambitious ventures with Tesla and SpaceX, but his journey wasn't always smooth. He repeatedly stepped out of his comfort zone, moving from software (PayPal) to electric vehicles, space exploration, and even neurotechnology (Neuralink). Musk's willingness to embrace the growth zone despite the risks and challenges has allowed him to make a significant impact in multiple industries.

- **Oprah Winfrey's Transition from Talk Show Host to Media Mogul.** Oprah Winfrey could have stayed in her comfort zone as a successful talk show host, but she chose to challenge herself by expanding her brand into a multimedia empire. This involved stepping into unfamiliar territory, such as launching her own television network (OWN) and producing films. By continuously pushing herself beyond her comfort zone, Oprah has built an enduring legacy and influenced millions.

- **J.K. Rowling's Leap of Faith.** Before becoming a literary sensation, J.K. Rowling was a single mother struggling to make ends meet. She had a passion for writing, but turning her manuscript into a published book required her to step out of her comfort zone and face countless rejections from publishers. By persevering through the uncertainty, Rowling eventually achieved unprecedented success with the *Harry Potter* series.

The Long-Term Benefits of Living in the Growth Zone

Living in the growth zone isn't just about tackling new challenges; it's about adopting a mindset that values growth, learning, and resilience. Over time, this mindset can transform your life in meaningful ways:

- **Increased Resilience.** Facing challenges regularly builds resilience, making you better equipped to handle future setbacks.

- **Greater Self-Awareness.** Pushing yourself beyond your limits allows you to learn more about who you are, your strengths, and areas for improvement.

- **Personal and Professional Development.** The skills and experiences gained in the growth zone enhance your qualifications and open up new career and personal opportunities.

- **Long-Term Fulfillment:** Achieving meaningful goals and personal growth leads to a sense of fulfillment that can't be found in a life confined to the comfort zone.

The Balance Between Comfort and Growth

While it's important to recognize the value of your comfort zone as a place for rest and recharge, it's equally essential to embrace the growth zone as the space where real development occurs. By finding a balance between these two states, you can live a life of ongoing growth while still maintaining the security and stability you need to stay grounded. Remember, every time you step out of your comfort zone, you're expanding the boundaries of what's possible for you.

Winnie the Pooh's wisdom encourages us to leave our cozy spots and explore the world. By stepping out of our comfort zones, we open ourselves to new experiences, personal growth, and meaningful connections. Whether in our personal lives or in business, being willing to embrace uncertainty and take risks can lead to amazing achievements and a more fulfilling life. Remember, growth happens when we push our limits and venture beyond what's familiar. So, take a lesson from Pooh: step out of your corner of the Forest and start the adventure of growth and discovery. The world is full of opportunities just waiting for you.

Never, Ever, Quit

"If the string breaks, then we try another piece of string."

Owl

Winnie the Pooh and his friends often find themselves in situations where things don't go as planned. In one story, Owl, the wise and practical bird, shares the above simple yet meaningful piece of advice. This quote captures the essence of resilience, discipline, and consistency. It reminds us how important it is to keep going when we face challenges and to value the effort of trying again after setbacks.

In Pooh's world, problems are often solved with creativity, teamwork, and a lot of trial and error.

For example, one day, Pooh and his friends tried to build a kite. Despite their best efforts, the string kept breaking. Instead of giving up, Owl's wise advice to try another piece of string encouraged them to keep going. They found a stronger string and eventually flew the kite successfully.

Persistence and a willingness to try again are essential for overcoming obstacles.

The Importance of Resilience, Discipline, and Consistency

Resilience is the ability to bounce back quickly from difficulties. It means recovering from setbacks and continuing to move forward despite challenges. Life is full of surprises that can disrupt our plans, but resilience helps us handle these obstacles and come out stronger. Discipline involves staying focused and committed to a task or goal, even when it gets tough. It requires self-control and the ability to stay motivated over time. Discipline is crucial for achieving long-term success, as it keeps us on track despite distractions and temptations. Consistency means regularly taking actions that support our goals. It's the small, steady efforts that lead to significant achievements. Consistency builds habits, and habits are the foundation of lasting progress and success.

It is these three qualities that are the crux of success. Granted, motivation tends to get a lot of the attention and is often in the spotlight, but, by definition, motivation rarely shows up when you need it most. The 'rah-rah' motivators tend to be a lot of hot air and hyperbole.

Take Winston Churchill for example.....

Winston Churchill, the famous British Prime Minister, showed resilience, discipline, and consistency throughout his life. His leadership during World War II especially highlighted these qualities in action.

- **Perseverance and Determination.** Churchill's career included both great successes and notable failures. Despite facing many setbacks, his strong determination remained steady. He believed that success often comes from pushing through tough times and never giving up, even when the odds seem impossible. During World War II, his leadership was vital in encouraging the British people to stay strong and keep fighting against Nazi Germany, despite the huge challenges they faced. His famous quote, *"Never, ever, ever give up,"* echoes Owl's advice to try another piece of string when the first one breaks.

- **Learn from Failure.** Churchill faced many setbacks in his career, including political losses and military mistakes. However, he viewed failure not as a dead end but as a chance to learn. By looking closely at his mistakes and understanding what went wrong, Churchill was able to make better choices in the future. This mindset helped him come back stronger after each failure, ultimately leading to his successful leadership during some of the most critical moments in history. Just as Pooh and his friends tried different strings until they found one that worked, Churchill's willingness to learn and adapt was key to his resilience.

- **Courage and Boldness.** Courage was a key part of Churchill's character. He often had to make tough and unpopular decisions, like opposing the appeasement of Hitler when many in the British government supported it. Churchill knew that true leadership requires the courage to take risks and make bold choices, even when facing criticism and uncertainty. His speeches and actions during World War II inspired not only his fellow countrymen but also people around the world to stand up against tyranny and fight for freedom. This boldness and courage are similar to trying a new piece of string, even when it's unsure if it will hold.

- **Adaptability and Change.** Churchill's ability to adapt and embrace change was clear throughout his career. He navigated through various roles, from military officer to political leader, and adjusted his strategies based on changing circumstances. His willingness to evolve and try new ideas was vital for his personal growth and effective leadership. Churchill understood that sticking to old methods and resisting change could slow progress, so he encouraged continuous improvement and innovation. This adaptability matches Owl's advice to keep trying different solutions until one works.

- **Vision and Clarity of Purpose.** Churchill had a deep understanding of what he wanted to achieve and communicated this vision clearly to inspire others. During World War II, his vision of a free and peaceful world guided his decisions and actions, helping to unite the British people and their allies in the fight against fascism. Churchill's ability to express his goals and motivate others to share in his vision was a key part of his success as a leader. His strong sense of purpose pushed him to keep going, no matter how many challenges he faced.

Resilience, discipline, and consistency are fundamental traits that can significantly influence success in both personal and professional endeavors. They help us navigate challenges, recover from setbacks, and stay committed to our goals. Whether it's striving for personal achievements like weight loss, building meaningful relationships, or reaching career milestones, these qualities serve as pillars that support our growth and progress. Understanding how to apply these lessons in practical ways can make all the difference in turning aspirations into reality.

- **Embracing Resilience in Personal Development.** In our personal lives, resilience enables us to bounce back from setbacks, adapt to changing circumstances, and maintain a positive outlook even in the face of adversity. For example, someone pursuing a fitness goal, like losing weight or gaining muscle, may encounter numerous challenges along the way—injuries, plateaus, or lifestyle changes that make it difficult to stay on track. The key is not to see these obstacles as failures but as opportunities to learn and adapt.

Practical Steps for Building Resilience

- **Set Realistic, Incremental Goals**. Break down your big goal into smaller, achievable milestones. This helps you celebrate progress along the way and reduces the risk of feeling overwhelmed. For instance, instead of setting a goal to lose 30 pounds, aim to lose 5 pounds per month. Each small victory reinforces your resilience and motivates you to keep going.

- **Develop a "Plan B" Mentality**. Expect that things won't always go according to plan. Instead of being discouraged by setbacks, prepare yourself by having alternative strategies. If your primary workout routine isn't delivering the results you want, for example, try a different form of exercise like swimming, yoga, or strength training.

- **Reflect on Past Resilience**. Think about times when you overcame difficulties in the past. What strategies did you use? How did you stay motivated? By recalling previous experiences, you can build confidence in your ability to overcome current challenges.

- **Practice Self-Compassion**. Be kind to yourself when you face setbacks. Understand that failure is a part of growth, and avoid harsh self-criticism. Instead, view setbacks as temporary and a natural part of the learning process.

- **Building Discipline Through Daily Habits.** Discipline is the ability to stay committed to your goals, even when you don't feel motivated. It's about consistently taking the necessary actions that move you closer to your objectives, regardless of whether you're in the mood to do so. For example, if you're trying to improve your health, discipline means sticking to your workout routine and meal plan even on days when you don't feel like it. It's the habit of making healthy choices over time that leads to long-term results. Here are some practical steps for cultivating discipline:

  - **Create a Daily Routine**. Establish a routine that aligns with your goals and stick to it. If you want to write a book, for instance, set aside time every morning to write, even if it's just for 15 minutes. The consistency of this routine will help reinforce your discipline.

- **Use a Habit Tracker**. A habit tracker can help you stay accountable and measure your progress. By visually tracking your daily actions, you can see your improvements over time and feel more motivated to maintain your efforts. Apps like HabitBull or even a simple calendar can be used to mark off days when you've completed a specific task, like exercising or practicing a skill.

- **Eliminate Temptations**. If you're trying to eat healthier, don't keep junk food in your house. If you want to reduce screen time, set your phone to "Do Not Disturb" mode during certain hours. Make it easier to stay disciplined by removing obstacles that can derail your progress.

- **Reward Yourself for Consistency**. Set up a reward system for maintaining discipline. For example, after exercising for 30 consecutive days, treat yourself to something you enjoy, like a massage or a new piece of workout gear. Positive reinforcement can help motivate you to continue making disciplined choices.

- **Staying Consistent to Achieve Long-Term Success.** Consistency is about showing up and putting in the effort day after day, even when the results aren't immediately visible. It's the small, repeated actions that compound over time to produce significant outcomes. In the case of weight loss, for example, consistently maintaining a calorie deficit and regular exercise will eventually lead to results, even if progress feels slow at first. The same principle applies to learning a new skill or mastering a craft; regular, focused practice is the key to improvement.

To Maintain Consistency

- **Focus on Progress, Not Perfection:** It's easy to get discouraged if you're not seeing rapid results. Instead of aiming for perfection, focus on making gradual progress. Remember, even small improvements add up over time.

- **Set "Non-Negotiables" in Your Schedule:** Make certain activities non-negotiable parts of your daily routine. For example, if you're working on a new skill, commit to practicing it for at least 20 minutes each day. Treat this time as sacred, and don't let other tasks interfere.

- **Use the "Two-Day Rule":** This rule suggests that you never skip more than one day in a row when working toward a goal. If you miss a workout, that's okay—but don't let yourself miss two consecutive days. This helps you stay consistent without feeling like you've failed when life gets in the way.

- **Track Your Wins and Losses:** Keep a journal where you document your progress and any setbacks. This can help you identify patterns and adjust your approach. Reviewing your entries regularly can also serve as a reminder of how far you've come and motivate you to stay on track.

Resilience, Discipline, and Consistency in Business

These qualities are just as crucial in the world of business, where setbacks and failures are part of the entrepreneurial journey. Success in business often requires facing rejection, learning from mistakes, and having the discipline to push forward when results are not guaranteed.

Examples of Resilience in Business

- **Colonel Harland Sanders (KFC)**. Colonel Sanders faced rejection after rejection when trying to sell his fried chicken recipe to restaurants. Despite over 1,000 rejections, he persisted because he believed in the quality of his product. His resilience eventually paid off when a restaurant owner took a chance on him, leading to the creation of one of the most famous fast-food chains in the world. Sanders' story shows that the willingness to keep trying, despite setbacks, is often what separates those who succeed from those who give up.

- **J.K. Rowling (Harry Potter Series)**. Before becoming one of the most successful authors in history, J.K. Rowling faced numerous rejections from publishers. She could have given up after the first few rejections, but she didn't. Her discipline to keep submitting her manuscript and the resilience to handle rejection ultimately led to the publication of the *Harry Potter* series, which became a global phenomenon.

- **Elon Musk (SpaceX and Tesla)**. Elon Musk faced numerous challenges and failures with both SpaceX and Tesla, including rockets that exploded on the launchpad and cars that didn't meet production targets. Yet, he maintained the discipline to keep innovating and the resilience to face public skepticism. Today, his companies are pioneers in their respective industries, demonstrating the power of resilience and persistence.

Practical Steps for Applying These Lessons in Business

- **Embrace a Growth Mindset**. Cultivate a mindset that views setbacks as opportunities to learn and grow. When facing a business challenge, ask yourself, "What can I learn from this experience, and how can I use it to improve?"

- **Implement the "Fail Fast, Learn Faster" Approach**. In business, failure is often inevitable. Instead of fearing failure, focus on failing quickly and learning from those experiences to improve your approach. Many successful entrepreneurs have adopted this mindset to iterate and refine their products or services rapidly.

- **Set Long-Term and Short-Term Goals**. Balance your long-term vision with short-term goals that keep you motivated. For instance, if you're aiming to expand your business, set monthly targets for new clients or revenue growth. This gives you something concrete to work toward while keeping the bigger picture in mind.

- **Establish Consistent Routines for Business Growth**. Whether it's daily team meetings, weekly progress reviews, or monthly strategy sessions, consistency in business operations can help build momentum and ensure that everyone is aligned with the company's objectives. These routines create a framework for accountability and continuous improvement.

The Compounding Effect of Small Actions

The concept of the compounding effect teaches us that small, consistent actions over time lead to significant results. Just like saving a little bit of money regularly can lead to a substantial sum through compound interest, taking small daily actions toward your goals can create a profound impact over time.

How to Leverage the Compounding Effect

- **Start Small but Start Now**. Even if you only have five minutes to dedicate to a new habit, start today. Those small daily efforts will add up over time. For instance, if you're trying to write a book, writing just one page a day means you'll have a 365-page manuscript by the end of the year.

- **Make It a Daily Habit**. Incorporate small habits into your routine that align with your goals. For example, if you want to improve your public speaking skills, practice speaking in front of a mirror for a few minutes every day.

- **Regularly Assess Your Progress**. Periodically review your progress to see how your small actions have accumulated over time. This can motivate you to keep going, and it also allows you to make adjustments to optimize your efforts.

The Strength of Another Piece of String

Owl's advice, *"If the string breaks, then we try another piece of string,"* is a powerful reminder that resilience, discipline, and consistency are key to overcoming life's challenges. By stepping out of our comfort zones, learning from failures, and keeping a clear vision, we can reach our goals and grow stronger along the way.

Winston Churchill's life and leadership reflect these qualities. His perseverance, adaptability, courage, and strong sense of purpose helped him lead through some of history's toughest times. By applying these principles in our own lives, we can face our challenges and continue striving for success and fulfillment. So, the next time your string breaks, remember Owl's wisdom: grab another piece of string. Keep trying, keep learning, and never give up!

Walking Away to Move Forward - The Art of Strategic Quitting

"I always get to where I'm going by walking away from where I have been."

Winnie the Pooh

This simple wisdom reminds us of the importance of moving forward, even if it means leaving something behind. Sometimes strategic quitting requires us to recognize when it's not just okay, but necessary, to quit, in order to achieve personal and professional growth.

Pooh and his friends often set off on new adventures. One day, Pooh visited Rabbit's house for honey but got stuck in the front door after eating too much. Despite Rabbit's initial attempts to push and pull him free, Pooh remains wedged in the doorway. Realizing that he is truly stuck and unable to move, Pooh has no choice but to wait until he becomes thinner again. His friends, including Christopher Robin, come to the conclusion that the only way to free Pooh is for him to go without food for a week so that he can slim down enough to fit through the doorway.

During this time, Pooh endures his hunger while his friends provide moral support. As the days pass, Pooh gradually becomes thin enough to be pulled free. Finally, with a concerted effort from his friends, Christopher Robin gives a strong pull, and Pooh is successfully freed from the doorway. This story illustrates the importance of patience, accepting help, and taking a different approach when faced with a seemingly insurmountable problem. In Pooh's case, he had to let go of immediate gratification (more honey) and make a sacrifice in order to get unstuck and move forward.

We all have a need to move forward and not stay stuck, even when it feels comfortable or familiar. Sometimes, we have to leave behind what's holding us back to reach where we truly need to be.

The Importance of Strategic Quitting

Contrary to the popular saying "Never quit," strategic quitting can actually be a useful tool for personal and professional growth. It means knowing when a situation is no longer benefiting you and having the courage to let it go, even when it's tough.

Here's why quitting can sometimes be the best choice:

- **Avoiding Futility**. Continuing to do something pointless, like pushing wet noodles up a hill, only leads to frustration and wasted effort.

- **Sunk Cost Fallacy**. The more we put into something, the harder it becomes to walk away, even when it's clearly not working. This mental trap keeps us stuck in unproductive efforts.

- **Focusing on Future Success**. The past is behind us, and no amount of effort will change it. It's better to focus on the future and make decisions that lead to long-term success.

Here's a few examples of the importance of strategic quitting in business....

Steven Bartlett. Steven Bartlett, co-founder and former CEO of Social Chain, offers a modern example of strategic quitting. At just 22, he built a multi-million-dollar business, but in 2020, at the height of its success, he decided to step down. In a conversation with YouTuber Ali Abdaal, Bartlett explained, *"What I realized was my edge was quitting faster than others, with peace and ease."* This shows the power of quitting strategically to create space for new opportunities. In his book *'Happy Sexy Millionaire: Unexpected Truths about Fulfillment, Love, and Success'*, Bartlett provides a guide for quitting. He suggests asking two important questions: are you thinking about quitting because it's too difficult?; and, are you thinking about quitting because it's mentally and emotionally draining? If the challenges outweigh the potential benefits, or if the situation is wearing you down with no improvement in sight, it may be time to quit.

Steve Jobs. Steve Jobs, co-founder of Apple Inc., is a great example of someone who understood the value of strategic quitting. In 1985, Jobs was famously forced out of the company he helped start. While this could have been a career-ending event, Jobs didn't see it as the end. Instead, he saw it as a chance to move on and start something new. Jobs went on to create NeXT, a computer platform company, and bought a small animation studio that would later become Pixar. These ventures allowed him to explore fresh ideas and technologies. His time away from Apple wasn't wasted; it was a period of growth and innovation. When he returned to Apple in 1997, he brought back valuable experiences that helped revitalize the company, leading to the creation of iconic products like the iMac, iPod, iPhone, and iPad.

J.K. Rowling. Before becoming a global sensation with the Harry Potter series, J.K. Rowling faced multiple rejections. Her manuscript was rejected by 12 publishers before Bloomsbury finally took a chance on her. But Rowling's story isn't just about perseverance through rejection, it's also about strategic quitting. Rowling once had a stable job, but it didn't fulfill her. She made the bold decision to quit and focus on her writing, despite the financial risks. This choice to leave a secure but unfulfilling career allowed her to dedicate herself fully to creating the Harry Potter world. Her decision to quit what wasn't working led to the pursuit of her true passion, bringing her immense success and personal fulfillment.

Elon Musk. Elon Musk, famous for his work with Tesla and SpaceX, also knows how important it is to quit strategically. Before achieving success with these companies, Musk helped start X.com, which later became PayPal. When PayPal was sold to eBay, Musk could have stayed on with the company, but he decided to leave. This smart choice allowed Musk to focus on his bigger dreams of sustainable energy and space exploration. By leaving PayPal, Musk opened up his time and energy to create Tesla and SpaceX, companies that are now leaders in their fields.

Techniques for Strategic Quitting

To practice strategic quitting effectively, consider these techniques:

- **Evaluate Effort vs. Reward**. Think about whether the effort you're putting into a project matches the possible rewards. If it doesn't, it might be time to move on.

- **Consider Mental and Emotional Impact**. If a task is causing a lot of stress without any clear benefits, it's worth reevaluating your commitment.

- **Seek Objective Feedback**. Our emotions can cloud our judgment. Ask trusted friends or mentors for their honest opinions, as they can offer a clearer view.

- **Set Clear Boundaries and Goals**. Define what success means to you and set limits. If a project or situation often crosses these limits, it may be time to quit.

- **Embrace a Growth Mindset**. See quitting as a way to grow rather than a failure. Every time you let go of something that isn't working, you create space for new opportunities and learning.

Quitting Strategically vs. Just Giving Up

It's important to understand the difference between quitting with a plan and simply giving up. Dr. Jordan B. Peterson highlights this idea well. He advises asking yourself if the new direction you're considering is just as hard or harder than the one you're leaving behind. This way, you can make sure you're choosing thoughtfully instead of just avoiding challenges. While quitting often gets a bad reputation, it can actually be a valuable skill. By quitting with intention, we can shift towards more rewarding careers and life choices. It's about trusting your gut and going after what feels right to you. Quitting takes just as much courage and thought as starting something new, but it can lead to the success you've always dreamed of.

The Power of Walking Away

Winnie the Pooh's saying, *"I always get to where I'm going by walking away from where I have been,"* reminds us of the value of knowing when to quit. By recognizing when something isn't helping us anymore and having the courage to move on, we can find greater success and happiness. Remember, quitting doesn't mean giving up on our dreams; it means being brave enough to change our approach and stay focused on our goals. So, don't hesitate to let go of what isn't working. Embrace the discomfort of moving forward, learn from your past, and trust that each step away from the past leads to a brighter future.

BOUNCING BACK — LESSONS FROM TIGGER AND BEYOND

"Life is not about how fast you run or how high you climb but how well you bounce."

Tigger

The Wisdom of Tigger

Tigger was known for his endless energy and his ability to bounce back from anything. One day, while teaching Roo how to bounce as high as possible, Tigger paused to share some wisdom.

"Life isn't about how fast you run or how high you climb, it's about how well you bounce," Tigger said with a big, cheerful grin.

Roo looked confused. *"What do you mean, Tigger?"*

"Well, little buddy," Tigger explained, *"it's not about how quickly you reach the top or how high you jump. It's about being able to get back up when you fall. That's what really counts."*

Tigger is known for his energy, optimism, and ability to "bounce" back from any situation. His approach to life reflects the core principles of resilience:

Tigger's wisdom teaches us that setbacks and challenges are inevitable, but the key to success is how well we recover from them. When life knocks us down, resilience allows us to get back up and keep moving forward. It's not about avoiding failure; it's about having the strength to rise again each time we stumble. Like Tigger, we can develop a "bounce-back" mentality by embracing challenges as opportunities to grow. Each time we overcome an obstacle, we build the confidence needed to tackle even bigger challenges in the future.

The Importance of Resilience

Tigger's words capture a key truth about life: resilience is essential. Resilience means being able to bounce back from difficulties, to recover quickly, and to keep moving forward despite setbacks. In our fast-paced, unpredictable world, resilience is more important than ever.

Take J.K. Rowling again. Before she became famous, Rowling faced countless rejections from publishers. She was a single mother living on welfare, struggling to get by. Yet, despite these challenges, she kept writing, driven by her love for storytelling and her belief in her work. Her resilience paid off. After many rejections, she finally found a publisher for Harry Potter, and the rest is history. Rowling's story shows the power of bouncing back and not giving up.

The Role of Consistency and Discipline

While resilience is about bouncing back, consistency and discipline are about sticking with it. These qualities are often more reliable than motivation, which can come and go. Consistency and discipline keep you moving toward your goals, even when motivation fades.

A study published in the European Journal of Social Psychology found that it takes about 66 days to form a new habit. This highlights the importance of consistency and discipline in reaching long-term goals. When you steadily work on building a habit, you set the foundation for success. This disciplined approach is more reliable than waiting for motivation to kick in.

Dwayne "The Rock" Johnson is a great example of how consistency and discipline lead to success. His intense workout routine and disciplined approach to his career have made him one of the highest-paid actors in Hollywood. He often shares how he wakes up before dawn to train and prepare for the day. His success is not just due to his talent but also to his unwavering consistency and discipline.

Why Resilience, Consistency, and Discipline Matter More Than Motivation

Motivation is often seen as the key to success, but it's not always dependable. One day it's there, and the next day it's gone. This is why resilience, consistency, and discipline are so important, they keep you moving forward even when motivation is low.

A study by the American Psychological Association found that people who relied on discipline, rather than motivation, were more likely to achieve their long-term goals. The research showed that discipline helped them stay committed even when they faced challenges, while those who relied only on motivation often gave up when obstacles arose.

The Science Behind Bouncing Back

Resilience, or the ability to recover from setbacks and adapt to challenging situations, is not a fixed trait—it can be cultivated and strengthened over time. Neuroscience provides compelling evidence that resilience can be developed through consistent practice and intentional behaviors. When we regularly confront and overcome challenges, our brains undergo changes that make us better equipped to handle future stress. This remarkable adaptability is known as neuroplasticity, the brain's ability to reorganize itself by forming new neural connections throughout life. Neuroplasticity allows us to learn new skills, recover from brain injuries, and, crucially, build resilience.

The Role of Neuroplasticity in Resilience

When we face challenges, our brain adapts by strengthening specific pathways that improve our ability to manage stress. Neuroplasticity enables the brain to change its structure and function in response to experiences, allowing us to become more resilient over time. This means that each time we encounter and overcome difficulties, we are literally rewiring our brains to be better prepared for future adversities.

The Hippocampus and Prefrontal Cortex are Two Key Areas of the Brain Involved in Resilience

- **The Hippocampus.** Which is responsible for memory and learning. When we experience stress, the hippocampus plays a role in processing those experiences and storing them as memories. A study from the University of California, Berkeley found that manageable levels of stress can actually stimulate neural growth in the hippocampus. This growth enhances cognitive functions such as memory retention and problem-solving, which in turn contribute to stronger emotional resilience.

- **The Prefrontal Cortex (PFC).** Which is located at the front of the brain, is crucial for decision-making, problem-solving, and emotion regulation. It helps us stay focused, think logically, and manage our emotional responses. Research shows that resilient individuals tend to have a more active and stronger prefrontal cortex, which enables them to cope with stress and adversity more effectively. When we encounter stressors, the prefrontal cortex helps us evaluate the situation, make informed decisions, and execute appropriate coping strategies. This ability to regulate emotions and stay calm under pressure is a hallmark of resilience.

The Power of Moderate Stress: Building Resilience Through Challenge

Interestingly, research indicates that moderate stress, when experienced in manageable doses, can actually be beneficial for building resilience. This concept is sometimes referred to as the "stress inoculation effect." Just like a vaccine exposes the body to a small, manageable amount of a virus to build immunity, experiencing moderate stress can prepare the brain to handle larger stressors in the future.

In the University of California, Berkeley study mentioned earlier, researchers found that moderate stress led to increased connections between neurons in the prefrontal cortex. These stronger neural connections resulted in better decision-making abilities and emotional control, which are critical components of resilience.

The Yerkes-Dodson Law, a well-established psychological theory, supports the idea that moderate levels of arousal (or stress) can enhance performance. Too little stress may lead to complacency, while too much stress can cause overwhelm. However, moderate stress serves as a motivator that pushes us to adapt, learn, and grow.

The Benefits of Mindfulness and Cognitive Training

In addition to experiencing manageable stress, mindfulness and cognitive training exercises can significantly boost resilience by supporting neuroplasticity.

Mindfulness meditation, the practice of being fully present and aware in the moment, has been shown to have a positive effect on brain structure, particularly in areas associated with resilience. A study published in Frontiers in Human Neuroscience found that mindfulness meditation increases gray matter density in the prefrontal cortex and other brain areas involved in emotional regulation. The participants who practiced mindfulness reported lower stress levels, improved mood, and better emotional control.

- **Mindfulness Meditation Techniques.** Practices such as mindful breathing, body scans, and guided meditation can help individuals develop a more active prefrontal cortex by training the brain to focus on the present moment rather than being overwhelmed by stress.

- **The Default Mode Network (DMN).** Mindfulness also quiets the brain's "default mode network," a region involved in mind-wandering and self-referential thoughts. When the DMN is less active, people experience fewer negative thought patterns, which can contribute to enhanced resilience.

- **Cognitive-Behavioral Therapy (CBT) and Resilience.** Cognitive-behavioral therapy (CBT) is another effective approach to strengthening resilience. CBT focuses on changing negative thought patterns and encouraging positive behaviors, which helps rewire the brain for better emotional regulation.

- **Reframing Negative Thoughts.** Through CBT techniques, individuals learn to identify and challenge unhelpful thoughts and replace them with more constructive ones. This practice not only improves mood but also strengthens the brain's resilience pathways, making it easier to handle future challenges.

- **Coping Strategies.** CBT provides practical tools for managing stress, such as problem-solving techniques, relaxation exercises, and self-reflection. These strategies support neuroplasticity by training the brain to respond to stress in more adaptive ways.

The Impact of Physical Exercise on Resilience

Physical exercise is not only beneficial for physical health but also has a profound impact on mental resilience. Regular aerobic exercise stimulates the production of brain-derived neurotrophic factor (BDNF), a protein that supports the growth, survival, and differentiation of neurons.

Higher levels of BDNF are associated with improved mood, cognitive function, and resilience to stress. A study published in Psychiatry Research showed that individuals who engaged in regular aerobic exercise (such as running, swimming, or cycling) had greater resilience to stress and displayed a stronger capacity to bounce back from adversity.

Engaging in physical activities like yoga, running, or weight training can act as a buffer against stress by increasing the availability of neurotransmitters such as dopamine and serotonin, which enhance mood and emotional stability. Exercise-induced neuroplasticity makes the brain more adaptable and less reactive to future stressors.

Resilience: Learning from Life's Challenges

Long-term studies have provided valuable insights into how resilience is cultivated over the course of a lifetime. For example, a longitudinal study by the American Psychological Association (APA) followed participants from childhood into adulthood, tracking how they coped with various life challenges. The study found that individuals who faced and overcame difficulties early in life tended to develop stronger coping mechanisms and higher levels of resilience as adults.

The study highlighted that children who were taught to view setbacks as learning experiences (rather than failures) developed a growth mindset that carried into adulthood. This mindset made them more likely to embrace new challenges and adapt to changing circumstances. The presence of strong support systems—such as family, friends, or mentors—was found to be a significant factor in developing resilience. Those who had positive relationships during times of adversity were more likely to exhibit resilience and experience less psychological distress.

Applying Tigger's Wisdom in Real Life

How can you build resilience, consistency, and discipline in your own life? Here are a few practical steps:

- **Challenge Yourself Regularly.** Intentionally expose yourself to manageable levels of stress or discomfort. This could mean trying a new hobby, taking on a challenging work project, or practicing public speaking. By stepping out of your comfort zone, you stimulate neuroplasticity and strengthen resilience pathways.

- **Incorporate Mindfulness Practices.** Engage in mindfulness exercises, such as meditation or yoga, at least a few times a week. These practices can help improve emotional regulation and decrease stress by enhancing the brain's ability to focus and remain calm under pressure.

- **Stay Physically Active.** Incorporate regular physical exercise into your routine. Aim for at least 30 minutes of moderate to vigorous aerobic activity, such as running, swimming, or dancing, most days of the week. Exercise supports brain plasticity, boosts mood, and enhances the brain's ability to handle stress.

- **Seek Social Support.** Surround yourself with a strong support network. Building meaningful relationships can buffer against stress and provide emotional resilience during tough times. Don't hesitate to reach out to friends, family, or a mental health professional when you need help.

- **Practice Cognitive-Behavioral Techniques.** Use CBT strategies to challenge negative thought patterns and replace them with positive, constructive ones. For example, if you find yourself thinking, "I can't handle this," reframe it as, "This is challenging, but I have the skills to manage it."

- **Set Realistic Goals.** Break down your long-term goals into smaller, manageable tasks. This makes it easier to stay consistent and disciplined.

- **Develop a Routine.** Create a daily routine that includes time for working on your goals. Sticking to a routine helps strengthen discipline.

- **Embrace Failure.** Accept that setbacks are a normal part of the journey. Use them as learning experiences to build resilience.

- **Stay Positive.** Keep a positive attitude. Like Tigger, try to enjoy the process, not just the destination.

Embracing the Science of Resilience

The science behind resilience shows how our brains are not static; they are dynamic and capable of growth. Thanks to neuroplasticity, we can intentionally shape our ability to bounce back from adversity. By consistently facing challenges, practicing mindfulness, staying active, and developing strong support networks, we can strengthen the brain's resilience pathways and become more adaptable to life's ups and downs.

So, remember Tigger's advice: life is not just about how fast you run or how high you climb; it's about how well you bounce back. Your brain is more than capable of adapting and growing as you encounter challenges. Embrace the power of resilience, keep bouncing back, and know that every setback is an opportunity to grow stronger and wiser.

THE POWER OF EMPATHY AND SIMPLE ACTS OF KINDNESS

"I don't feel very much like Pooh today," said Pooh. *"There, there,"* said Piglet, *"I'll bring you tea and honey until you do."*

In this heartwarming moment between Pooh and Piglet, we find a simple yet profound lesson in empathy and friendship. Piglet's instinctive offer to bring tea and honey to his friend in need is more than just a kind gesture; it is an act of genuine compassion. Rather than trying to solve Pooh's sadness or offer advice, Piglet recognizes the importance of just being there, providing comfort in the form of a familiar, soothing ritual. His actions reflect a deep understanding of what Pooh needs most—emotional support and reassurance. This quiet but powerful moment shows us that real empathy is about recognizing a friend's feelings and responding with genuine care, even when there isn't a clear solution to their troubles.

Empathy is often described as the ability to put ourselves in another person's shoes, to see the world from their perspective and feel what they are feeling. It goes beyond sympathy, which is simply acknowledging someone else's emotions; empathy involves truly sharing in those emotions and responding with understanding. When Piglet brings Pooh tea and honey, he isn't just trying to distract Pooh from his sadness or cheer him up with treats. Instead, he is saying, *"I'm here for you, just as you are."* This kind of empathetic response doesn't aim to fix the situation but rather to offer comfort and companionship, letting Pooh know that he isn't alone. It's a reminder that sometimes, the most meaningful support we can provide is simply to be present.

The Healing Power of Presence

In today's world, where distractions abound and our attention is constantly pulled in different directions, the power of simply being there for someone is often underestimated. Yet, Piglet's choice to sit with Pooh and offer tea and honey emphasizes the significance of being fully present. It reassures Pooh that his feelings are recognized and that he has a friend by his side, no matter what. This quiet companionship sends a powerful message: *"You are not alone."* The value of presence lies not in offering solutions but in providing a safe space where someone can feel seen, heard, and understood. By choosing to stay by Pooh's side, Piglet shows us that true friendship often means setting aside our own need to "fix" things and instead offering our time, attention, and a listening ear.

In many ways, Piglet's response mirrors an important principle found in therapeutic practices—active listening. When we truly listen to someone, we validate their experiences and emotions. We don't interrupt, judge, or try to immediately fix their problems. This form of empathy creates a bridge between people, fostering deeper connections and mutual trust. In the story of Pooh and Piglet, this bond is strengthened not through grand gestures, but through the small act of sharing a comforting moment. It is a powerful reminder that sometimes, healing can begin with a simple gesture, like a cup of tea and a kind word.

The Power of Small, Thoughtful Gestures

Throughout Winnie the Pooh's adventures, the theme of finding comfort in life's simple pleasures frequently appears. Whether it's sharing a pot of honey, taking a walk through the Hundred Acre Wood, or just sitting quietly together, these small acts of kindness often hold the greatest power to heal and uplift. When Piglet brings Pooh tea and honey, he acknowledges the therapeutic potential of simplicity. He understands that comfort doesn't have to come in the form of elaborate solutions or profound advice; sometimes, it's the small, thoughtful gestures that remind us we are cared for. This idea challenges the notion that only big, dramatic actions can make a difference, suggesting instead that even the smallest act of kindness can have a profound impact on someone's well-being.

Psychologists have long studied the benefits of small, compassionate acts on mental health. Research shows that small gestures of kindness can create a ripple effect, enhancing both the giver's and receiver's sense of well-being. These acts don't have to be grand or complicated to be meaningful. As in the case of Pooh and Piglet, the simple offering of tea and honey carries with it a message of love, understanding, and solidarity. It shows us that we don't need to wait for the "right" moment to help someone feel better; we can start with something as simple as a kind word or a comforting presence.

Empathy as the Foundation of True Friendship

Empathy in friendships goes beyond shared interests or mutual experiences—it is the cornerstone of a deep, lasting connection. When friends are truly empathetic, they create an environment where both feel safe to express their vulnerabilities. This type of relationship is built on trust, where each friend knows they can count on the other during tough times. Piglet's willingness to comfort Pooh not only provides immediate relief but also strengthens the foundation of their friendship. It shows that friendship isn't about always being able to solve each other's problems, but about offering unwavering support and care.

The story of Pooh and Piglet serves as a reminder that being emotionally available for someone doesn't necessarily mean having all the answers. Often, the most important thing we can offer is our presence and understanding. As friendships deepen, the bonds formed through acts of empathy and kindness create a resilient network of support that can withstand life's inevitable ups and downs. Piglet's empathy reinforces the idea that the most enduring friendships are those where each person feels valued, accepted, and loved just as they are, without the pressure to always be happy or perfect.

Learning from Historical Insights on Friendship

The wisdom found in the friendship between Pooh and Piglet echoes through the words of historical figures who understood the essence of true companionship. Muhammad Ali once remarked, *"Friendship... is not something you learn in school. But if you haven't learned the meaning of friendship, you really haven't learned anything."* His words remind us that life's most important lessons often lie not in academic achievements or professional successes, but in our capacity to care for and support each other. Piglet's kindness exemplifies this, teaching us that understanding and compassion are at the heart of every meaningful friendship.

Similarly, Euripides, the ancient Greek playwright, said, *"One loyal friend is worth ten thousand relatives."* Piglet's loyalty to Pooh is evident in his actions, showing that genuine friendship is a choice and a commitment. It is built on daily acts of kindness and support that reinforce the trust between two individuals. The bond between Pooh and Piglet is not sustained by grand declarations or dramatic gestures but by the quiet, consistent presence that is there even in the smallest moments.

Bringing Out the Best in Each Other

Friendships like that of Pooh and Piglet do more than provide comfort; they help us grow and bring out the best in each other. As Henry Ford famously said, *"My best friend is the one who brings out the best in me."* Piglet's ability to recognize Pooh's need and respond with compassion is an example of how true friends can help each other navigate life's challenges. When we approach our friendships with empathy, we empower those we care about to overcome their struggles, reminding them that they are not defined by their moments of weakness but by the strength they find in companionship.

Cultivating a World of Empathy and Kindness

The enduring friendship between Pooh and Piglet teaches us invaluable lessons about the power of empathy, the beauty of small gestures, and the importance of simply being there for one another. As we reflect on these lessons, we are encouraged to bring these values into our daily lives. Whether it's listening without judgment, showing loyalty through consistent acts of kindness, or finding joy in life's simplest pleasures, these principles guide us in building deeper and more meaningful relationships.

By choosing to embrace empathy, presence, and simplicity in our interactions, we can foster a world where acts of kindness are the norm, not the exception. As we navigate our own lives, let the quiet wisdom of the Hundred Acre Wood remind us that sometimes, the greatest comfort can be found in the smallest gestures—a cup of tea, a kind word, or the silent reassurance that we are not alone.

LESSONS IN PERSONAL BRANDING FROM WINNIE THE POOH

In the Hundred Acre Wood, simplicity is at the heart of everything. Winnie the Pooh's gentle wisdom and down-to-earth nature offer more than just lessons about friendship and honey; they provide valuable insights into building a personal brand that feels authentic, approachable, and impactful. Whether you're a professional, a creative, or an entrepreneur, the principles that guide Pooh's life can help you shape a personal brand that resonates with others and stands the test of time.

Insight No. 1 — Embrace Clarity

Pooh's approach to communication is simple and clear. He uses language that is easy to understand, reminding us that clarity is key in personal branding. Your personal brand message should be straightforward and accessible, avoiding jargon or complicated language that might confuse your audience. Whether you're creating a LinkedIn profile, writing a blog, or introducing yourself at a networking event, aim for simplicity. Your message should communicate who you are and what you stand for in a way that resonates with people.

- **Pooh's World.** In one of his adventures, Pooh asked Piglet, *"What about lunch?"* It's a simple, direct question that leaves no room for misunderstanding. In your personal branding, aim to be equally clear. For example, if you're a writer, describe yourself as "a storyteller who brings ideas to life," rather than using industry jargon like "content strategist and narrative architect."

- **Real World Example.** Think about Richard Branson's personal brand. His communication style is simple and relatable, even when talking about complex topics like entrepreneurship and innovation. His authenticity and clear messaging make him approachable, which is a significant part of his brand's appeal.

Practical Steps

- **Identify Your Core Message.** What do you want people to know about you? Define your key message in one sentence and use it as a guiding statement for all your communications.

- **Avoid Jargon.** Use language that a wide audience can understand. If you're tempted to use technical terms, consider whether there's a simpler way to express your point.

- **Be Direct.** When communicating your value, be concise and specific. Instead of saying, "I assist businesses with optimizing their operational efficiencies," try, "I help businesses save time and reduce costs."

Insight No. 2 — Define Your Vision

Pooh wisely says, *"Before beginning a Hunt, it is wise to ask someone what you are looking for before you begin looking for it."* The same goes for personal branding. Before you start shaping your brand, it's important to have a clear vision of what you want to achieve. Your vision should be your guiding star, helping you make decisions that align with your long-term goals.

- **Pooh's World.** When Pooh and his friends set out to find honey, they know exactly what they're after. This clear goal shapes their actions and keeps them focused. Similarly, having a well-defined vision for your personal brand ensures that all your efforts are pointed in the right direction.

- **Real World Example.** Simon Sinek's personal brand revolves around his vision of inspiring others to find their "Why." His TED Talk on the topic and his book, *Start With Why*, are both consistent with his vision, making him a thought leader in the field of leadership and purpose-driven success.

Practical Steps

- **Set Specific Goals.** What do you want to be known for? Whether it's becoming an expert in a particular field, launching a new project, or influencing a specific audience, define your goals clearly.

- **Align Your Actions with Your Vision.** Make sure that everything you do—whether it's the content you create, the people you connect with, or the opportunities you pursue—aligns with your vision.

- **Review and Adjust.** Periodically revisit your vision to see if it still aligns with your goals. As you grow, your vision might evolve, and that's okay.

Insight No. 3 — Take Your Time

"Rivers know this: There is no hurry. We shall get there some day." Personal branding, like Pooh's approach to life, is a marathon, not a sprint. Building a strong brand requires patience, consistency, and steady progress. It's important to understand that success won't come overnight, and that's perfectly okay.

- **Pooh's World.** Pooh often takes the time to enjoy the journey rather than rushing to the destination. Similarly, personal branding is about the process of continually shaping and refining how you present yourself to the world.

- **Real World Example.** Brené Brown took years to build her reputation as a thought leader in vulnerability and courage. Her TED Talks, books, and social media presence were all developed over time, creating a consistent and impactful personal brand.

Practical Steps

- **Set Milestones Instead of Deadlines.** While having timelines can help keep you focused, be flexible. Focus on small wins and progress rather than rushing to achieve the end goal.

- **Consistency Over Intensity.** It's better to post meaningful content once a week consistently than to go all-in for a month and then disappear. Consistency helps in building credibility over time.

- **Embrace Slow Growth.** Remember that slow growth is still growth. The relationships you build, the skills you develop, and the experiences you gain will all contribute to your long-term success.

Insight No. 4 — Infuse Joy and Positivity

"Sometimes the smallest things take up the most room in your heart." Pooh finds joy in the simplest of things, and this sense of happiness is infectious. In personal branding, infusing positivity and sharing what brings you joy can help you connect with others on a deeper, emotional level. People are drawn to positive energy, so letting your personality and passions shine through can make you more relatable.

- **Pooh's World.** Whether it's finding joy in a pot of honey or enjoying a sunny day with friends, Pooh shows us that happiness can come from the simplest things. Let your brand reflect the things that bring you joy.

- **Real World Example.** Consider Ellen DeGeneres. Her brand is built around positivity, humor, and kindness. Her authenticity and joyful approach to life resonate with millions of people, making her one of the most relatable figures in entertainment.

Practical Steps

- **Share What You Love.** Whether it's through social media, blogs, or personal conversations, talk about the things that make you happy. It humanizes your brand and makes you more approachable.

- **Highlight Positive Stories.** Share your success stories, the lessons you've learned, and the challenges you've overcome with a positive spin.

- **Incorporate Humor.** Don't be afraid to let your sense of humor show. A little light-heartedness can go a long way in making you more relatable.

Insight No. 5 — Allow for Rest and Recharge

"People say nothing is impossible, but I do nothing every day." Pooh's wisdom reminds us of the importance of taking time to rest. Building a personal brand can be exhausting, and burnout can harm creativity and productivity. Make time to step back and recharge.

- **Pooh's World.** Pooh often pauses to take in his surroundings, enjoying quiet moments and recharging his energy. In personal branding, it's important to take breaks to maintain your creativity and motivation.

- **Real World Example.** Arianna Huffington is a strong advocate for the power of rest. After experiencing burnout firsthand, she launched the *Thrive Global* initiative to help people prioritize well-being and mental health.

Practical Steps

- **Set Boundaries.** Allocate time for rest and hobbies outside of your branding efforts. This will help you come back refreshed and more focused.

- **Schedule Breaks.** Treat breaks as part of your schedule. Block out time on your calendar for non-work activities, meditation, or simply doing nothing.

- **Listen to Your Body.** Pay attention to signs of fatigue or burnout and give yourself permission to step away when needed.

Insight No. 6 — Trust Simple Wisdom

"Those who are clever, who have a Brain, never understand anything." Overthinking can often get in the way of effective personal branding. Sometimes, the best approach is the simplest one. Trust your instincts and apply common sense to your branding decisions.

- **Pooh's World.** Pooh's solution to getting honey is simple—use a balloon. It may not be a complex plan, but it works. Sometimes, in personal branding, taking the straightforward path is more effective than trying to do something elaborate or complicated.

- **Real World Example.** Marie Kondo built her personal brand around a very simple idea: decluttering by keeping only the things that "spark joy." This common-sense approach resonated with millions and turned her into an international phenomenon.

Practical Steps

- **Stick to What Works.** If something has been working well for your personal brand, don't feel the need to complicate it. Sometimes, being simple and consistent is better.

- **Trust Your Gut.** If a particular decision feels right, even if it's unconventional, trust yourself. Your intuition can be a valuable guide.

- **Focus on Your Audience's Needs.** Think about what your audience really wants from you. Often, they are looking for clarity, relatability, and solutions, rather than complex jargon or flashy presentations.

Insight No. 7 — Show Passion and Purpose

"Some people care too much. I think it's called love." Passion can be a powerful driver of personal branding. When you genuinely care about what you do, it shows, and people are drawn to that energy.

- **Pooh's World.** Pooh's love for his friends and his dedication to finding honey are central to who he is. In the same way, your personal brand should reflect the things that you care deeply about.

- **Real World Example.** Gary Vaynerchuk is known for his passion and energy. His personal brand revolves around hustle, entrepreneurship, and authentic communication. His love for what he does is contagious, inspiring others to pursue their passions.

Practical Steps

- **Communicate Your "Why".** Share why you do what you do. Let your audience see the passion behind your work, whether it's through videos, blog posts, or speaking engagements.

- **Align Your Brand with Your Values.** Make sure that the causes you support and the projects you pursue align with your core beliefs and values. Authentic passion comes from working on things that matter to you.

- **Inspire Others.** Use your platform to motivate and inspire. Share stories of your own journey, including both successes and struggles, to show that you are genuinely committed to your purpose.

Insight No. 8 — Embrace Feedback and Learn

"You find sometimes that a Thing which seems very Thingish inside you is quite different when it gets out into the open and has other people looking at it." Feedback is a valuable tool in personal branding. It helps you see your brand from different perspectives, allowing you to improve and grow.

- **Pooh's World.** Pooh often receives feedback from his friends, which helps him see things in a new light. Similarly, when you receive constructive criticism, it's an opportunity for growth.

- **Real World Example.** Personal branding coach Dorie Clark encourages professionals to seek out feedback regularly to understand how they're being perceived and to make adjustments accordingly.

Practical Steps

- **Ask for Feedback.** Don't be afraid to reach out to your audience, mentors, or colleagues and ask for their thoughts on your personal brand.

- **Be Open to Change.** Use feedback to make improvements. Sometimes, a small change can make a big difference in how your brand is perceived.

- **Reflect and Adapt.** Take time to reflect on the feedback you receive and adapt your strategies accordingly. Personal branding is an ongoing process of growth and refinement.

Insight No. 9 — Connect Authentically with Others

"You can't stay in your corner of the Forest waiting for others to come to you. You have to go to them sometimes." Personal branding is about connecting with others, not just presenting an image. Build genuine relationships, engage with your audience, and be proactive in reaching out.

- **Pooh's World.** Pooh doesn't wait for his friends to come to him; he goes out to find them. This proactive approach strengthens his bonds with others.

- **Real World Example.** LinkedIn influencer Leah Turner has built her personal brand around authentic, meaningful engagement on the platform. Her willingness to connect and share openly has made her a trusted voice in her field.

Practical Steps

- **Engage with Your Community.** Don't just share content—interact with your audience by responding to comments, sharing other people's work, and joining relevant conversations.

- **Attend Networking Events.** Make an effort to attend events, either in person or online, where you can meet new people and expand your network.

- **Be Generous.** Offer help, share resources, and support others in their journey. The more you give, the more you'll get back in terms of meaningful connections.

The Bottom Line

The Wisdom of Pooh offers valuable lessons for personal branding. By embracing clarity, defining your vision, taking your time, infusing positivity, allowing for rest, trusting simple wisdom, showing passion, welcoming feedback, and connecting authentically, you can create a personal brand that resonates with others and stands out in a crowded world. Let Pooh's gentle and wise approach to life guide you in building a brand that's not just about presenting an image, but about sharing your true self with the world. After all, a personal brand built on authenticity and genuine connections is a brand that lasts.

APPLYING CLARITY AMIDST CHAOS

"Don't be ridikkerous,"

Tigger

In the midst of life's inevitable chaos, there's something refreshing about Tigger's carefree spirit. With his boundless energy and fearless optimism, Tigger has a way of cutting through life's clutter, allowing us to see the heart of what really matters. His famous line, *"Don't be ridikkerous,"* may sound like playful nonsense at first, but it carries a profound wisdom about staying grounded in the midst of distractions and complications. Tigger's approach isn't about ignoring the chaos or pretending it doesn't exist—it's about choosing not to get tangled up in it.

His lively, straightforward attitude offers a guiding light for finding clarity amidst the noise of modern life. Whether we're grappling with overwhelming tasks at work, navigating the complexities of relationships, or dealing with life's unexpected turns, Tigger's approach to "bouncing back" shows us that clarity is more than just seeing through the confusion. It's about staying true to what's important, letting go of the unnecessary, and meeting challenges head-on with resilience and joy.

Tigger's playful wisdom can be applied to different areas of our lives, helping us cut through distractions, simplify our focus, and embrace the path forward with confidence and purpose. From the workplace to personal relationships, and from overcoming setbacks to finding balance, these lessons show how a bit of Tigger's exuberance can help us tackle even the most daunting obstacles. As we adopt his clarity amidst chaos, we not only find our way—we rediscover the joy of the journey itself.

Insight No. 1 — Cutting Through the Noise in Professional Settings

- **Tigger's Approach**. Tigger doesn't get bogged down by unnecessary details or complications. He sees the big picture and focuses on what's important.

- **Application in the Workplace**. In today's fast-paced work environment, it's easy to feel overwhelmed by endless emails, meetings, and competing priorities. To apply Tigger's wisdom, start by identifying the main objectives of your role or project. What key outcomes do you need to achieve? By focusing on these priorities, you can avoid distractions from less important tasks. For example, if you're leading a team on a major project, use Tigger's approach to streamline your focus. Set clear, achievable goals and communicate these to your team. Encourage everyone to concentrate on the tasks that will drive the project forward, rather than getting sidetracked by minor issues. By cutting through the noise, you'll create a more efficient and productive work environment.

- **Practical Steps**.

  - **Prioritize Tasks**. Use tools like the Eisenhower Matrix to sort tasks by urgency and importance.

- **Clear Communication**. Regularly share the key objectives with your team to ensure everyone is aligned.

- **Simplify Processes**. Look for ways to simplify workflows and reduce unnecessary steps that add complexity.

Insight No. 2 — Embracing Clarity in Personal Relationships

- **Tigger's Approach**. Tigger's wisdom lies in his ability to see things as they are, not as they appear. He embraces simplicity and avoids overthinking.

- **Application to Personal Relationships**. Relationships with family, friends, or romantic partners can sometimes become complicated by misunderstandings and miscommunication. Applying Tigger's principle of clarity can help you maintain healthy and straightforward relationships.

- **Practical Steps**. This means addressing issues directly instead of letting them fester. If you're feeling hurt or confused by something a loved one has said or done, take a page from Tigger's book and have an open, honest conversation. Focus on understanding their perspective without making assumptions, and clearly express your own feelings. For example, if you've had a disagreement with a close friend, instead of overanalyzing their actions or words, approach them with a simple, direct question like, *"Can we talk about what happened?"* This approach encourages open dialogue and helps prevent small issues from growing into bigger problems.

  - **Communicate Openly**. Encourage regular, honest conversations with those you care about.

  - **Avoid Assumptions**. Ask questions to clarify instead of jumping to conclusions.

  - **Keep It Simple**. Focus on the core of the issue rather than getting lost in the details.

Insight No. 3 — Navigating Uncertainty with Confidence

- **Tigger's Approach**. Tigger never hesitates or doubts himself. When he sets a goal, he moves forward with confidence and energy.

- **Application in Career Growth**. In your career, you'll likely face moments of uncertainty, whether starting a new job, taking on a tough project, or making a career change. Tigger's unwavering confidence teaches an important lesson: believe in yourself and take bold action. For example, if you're thinking about a big career shift, like moving into a new field or starting your own business, it's normal to feel unsure. But by embracing Tigger's confidence, you can tackle this change with a positive mindset. Start by identifying your skills and strengths, then create a clear plan of action. Instead of being held back by fear of the unknown, take that first step toward your goal, trusting in your ability to adapt and succeed.

- **Practical Steps.**

    ○ **Self-Assessment**. Identify your key strengths and how they can apply to new opportunities.

    ○ **Goal Setting**. Break down your bigger career goals into smaller, achievable steps.

    ○ **Take Action**. Start with the first step, no matter how small, and build momentum from there.

Insight No. 4 — Balancing Work and Play

- **Tigger's Approach**. Tigger shows how to live with enthusiasm and balance, knowing when to work hard and when to enjoy life.

- **Application in Work-Life Balance**. Maintaining a balance between work and personal life is key to overall well-being. Tigger's playful spirit reminds us that life isn't just about reaching goals, it's also about enjoying the ride. To apply this, set clear boundaries between work and personal time. Just like Tigger enjoys bouncing and playing, find activities outside of work that make you happy and help you relax. Whether it's spending time with family, enjoying a hobby, or taking a walk, these joyful moments are important for recharging and keeping a positive mindset. For example, if you've been working long hours on a tough project, take regular breaks and make time for things you enjoy. By creating this balance, you'll return to work with more energy and a clearer mind, just like how Tigger approaches every new adventure with excitement.

- **Practical Steps.**

    ○ **Set Boundaries**. Decide on clear working hours and stick to them.

    ○ **Make Time for Joy**. Set aside time for activities that make you happy and help you relax.

- **Mindful Transition**s. Take a few moments to mentally shift between work and personal time to keep a healthy balance.

Insight No. 5 — Resilience in the Face of Adversity

- **Tigger's Approach**. Tigger's determination is unshakeable. When he faces challenges, he doesn't give up, he bounces back, both literally and figuratively.

- **Application in Personal Challenges**. Life is full of obstacles, from unexpected setbacks to ongoing struggles. Tigger's resilience shows us that while we can't always control what happens, we can control how we react. When facing tough times, it's easy to feel discouraged. But by adopting Tigger's resilient attitude, you can approach challenges with a positive mindset. Focus on what you can learn and how the experience can make you stronger. For example, if you're going through a difficult time, like losing a job or dealing with a health issue, think of Tigger: Don't get stuck on the setback. Instead, find ways to bounce back and keep moving forward.

- **Practical Steps**.

  - **Positive Mindset**. Try to see challenges as chances to grow.

  - **Learn from Setbacks**. Reflect on what each difficult experience can teach you.

  - **Keep Moving Forward**. Take small steps each day to overcome setbacks and move toward recovery.

Bouncing Toward a Purposeful Life

Tigger's wisdom, delivered with a playful bounce and a cheerful smile, offers deep lessons that help us navigate the complexities of life. Whether in our careers, relationships, or personal growth, Tigger's principles of clarity, confidence, balance, and resilience provide a guide for facing challenges with a positive, determined mindset.

By following Tigger's approach, we can cut through distractions, stay focused on what really matters, and face life's ups and downs with the same enthusiasm and joy Tigger brings to every bounce. As we apply these lessons to our lives, we find that finding clarity in the chaos isn't just possible, it's a path to success, fulfillment, and happiness.

Conquering Imaginary Foes: Lessons From Heffalumps and Woozles

"Heffalumps and Woozles steal honey... beware, beware!"

Winnie the Pooh

The Heffalumps and Woozles from Winnie the Pooh's world may be strange, whimsical creatures, but they represent something much more significant than just figments of a dream. For Pooh, these imaginary beings embody the fears, distractions, and doubts that often loom large in our minds. They symbolize the things that scare us, hold us back, or make us lose focus—things that feel real but are often exaggerated or even entirely made up.

In life, we all face our own Heffalumps and Woozles—those imaginary foes that fill our heads with doubts, worries, and distractions. They show up as self-doubt whispering that we're not good enough, as worries about failure keeping us from taking risks, or as distractions pulling us away from our true priorities. But just as Pooh ultimately realizes that the Heffalumps and Woozles are not real threats, we, too, can learn to see our fears and distractions for what they truly are: mental obstacles that we can overcome.

Lessons from these curious creatures can help us stay focused, manage our fears, and build resilience in the face of life's challenges. By understanding the Heffalumps and Woozles for what they are—products of our imagination—we can better navigate our lives with clarity and courage, and pursue our goals with a sense of purpose and joy.

Insight No. 1 — Overcoming Imaginary Fears in Professional Settings

- **Heffalumps and Woozles as Mental Constructs**. In Winnie the Pooh's dream, Heffalumps and Woozles seem mischievous and threatening, but they aren't real dangers. They are just products of the imagination, similar to the fears we often create in our own minds.

- **Application in the Workplace**. At work, fears like failing, being rejected, or feeling inadequate can hold us back, stopping us from taking risks or grabbing opportunities. These fears, like the Heffalumps and Woozles, are often blown out of proportion in our minds, leading to procrastination, self-doubt, and stagnation. For instance, if you're thinking about a career change or going for a promotion, the fear of not being good enough or of failing may stop you from trying. But by realizing that these fears are often bigger in your mind than in reality, you can step back and look at the situation clearly. Acknowledge the fear, but don't let it control your actions. Instead, focus on your strengths and growth potential, just like how Pooh realizes that the Heffalumps and Woozles aren't real threats.

- **Practical Steps**.
  - **Acknowledge the Fear**. Recognize when fear is influencing your choices. Name it, understand it, and put it into perspective.
  - **Take Action Despite Fear**. Let fear motivate you instead of stopping you.

Take small steps toward your goal, gaining confidence as you go.

- **Seek Support**. Talk to mentors, colleagues, or friends who can offer a balanced perspective and encourage you to keep moving forward.

Insight No. 2 — Managing Distractions in Personal and Professional Life

- **Heffalumps and Woozles as Distractions**. Just like how these imaginary creatures in Pooh's dream distract him from his love for honey, distractions in real life can pull us away from our true goals and dreams.

- **Application in Daily Life**. Distractions come in many forms, social media, constant notifications, cluttered environments, and even the chaos of everyday life. These distractions can break our focus and weaken our efforts, much like how the Heffalumps and Woozles take Pooh's attention away. Whether in personal or professional life, managing distractions is key to staying focused and productive. For example, think about your daily routine. If you're often interrupted by notifications or sidetracked by less important tasks, it's easy to lose sight of your main goals. By learning from Pooh, you can develop strategies to manage these distractions so they don't take you away from what really matters.

- **Practical Steps**.

  - **Set Clear Boundaries**. Set specific times for focused work and relaxation. Turn off notifications during work hours to avoid interruptions.

  - **Declutter Your Environment**. Keep your workspace organized and free from distractions. A clean space leads to a clear mind.

  - **Practice Mindfulness**. Use mindfulness techniques, like deep breathing or meditation, to focus your thoughts and reduce the impact of distractions.

Insight No. 3 — The Power of Perception – Conquering Self-Doubt

- **Heffalumps and Woozles as Symbols of Self-Doubt**. These creatures represent the doubts that sneak into our minds, making our fears seem bigger and harder to overcome.

- **Application in Personal Growth**. Self-doubt is a common barrier in both personal and professional growth. It can show up as imposter syndrome, the fear of not being good enough, or the belief that others are judging us harshly. Like the Heffalumps and Woozles, these doubts are often more about how we see things than how they really are. For instance, when starting a new project or learning a new skill, self-doubt can make you question your abilities and self-worth. But by recognizing that these doubts are often just in your mind, you can work to overcome them. Just as Pooh realizes the Heffalumps and Woozles aren't real threats, you can see that self-doubt is often an illusion, one you have the power to break.

- **Practical Steps**.

  - **Challenge Negative Thoughts**. When self-doubt appears, question if it's really true. Replace negative thoughts with positive affirmations.

  - **Celebrate Small Wins**. Recognize and celebrate your achievements, no matter how small. This builds confidence and helps push self-doubt aside.

  - **Visualize Success**. Imagine yourself succeeding. This boosts your positive mindset and weakens the power of doubt.

Insight No. 4 — Staying Focused on Your Goals

- **Heffalumps and Woozles as Goal Distractors**. In Pooh's dream, these creatures pull him away from his main goal, enjoying honey. Similarly, in life, distractions can make us lose sight of our goals.

- **Application in Goal Setting and Achievement**. Staying focused on your goals takes discipline and clarity, especially in a world full of distractions. The lesson from Pooh is clear: to reach your goals, you must not let imaginary foes or outside distractions steer you off course.For instance, if you've set a long-term goal, like starting a business or earning a degree, it's easy to feel overwhelmed by daily challenges and distractions. However, by keeping your eyes on the end goal, just like Pooh focuses on honey, you can handle these challenges more effectively. Break your goal into smaller, manageable steps, and don't let temporary setbacks or distractions derail your progress.

- **Practical Steps**.

  - **Set Clear, Achievable Goals**. Divide large goals into smaller tasks to keep moving forward and avoid feeling overwhelmed.

  - **Prioritize**. Focus on the tasks that directly help you reach your goal. Stay away from activities that don't match your objectives.

- **Regularly Review Progress**. Check your progress often to make sure you're on track and adjust your plan as needed.

Insight No. 5 — Building Resilience Against Fear and Distractions

- **Heffalumps and Woozles as Tests of Resilience**. These imaginary creatures challenge Pooh's ability to bounce back, just like how our fears and distractions challenge our determination in real life.

- **Applying Resilience in Our Lives**. Resilience means the ability to recover from setbacks and stay focused when facing difficulties. Just as Pooh learns to deal with his fears, we can also build resilience by realizing that many of our challenges aren't as scary as they appear. For example, if you face a setback, like a failed project or a personal disappointment, it's important to see it as a chance to learn instead of a failure. By building resilience, you can keep moving forward despite challenges, just like Pooh continues his adventures even after meeting the Heffalumps and Woozles.

- **Practical Steps**.

  - **Practice Gratitude**. Keep a gratitude journal to remind yourself of the good things in your life, which can help protect you from negative thoughts.

  - **Build a Support System**. Surround yourself with supportive friends, family, or colleagues who can help you stay strong and resilient.

  - **Learn from Setbacks**. View challenges as chances to grow. Think about what you can learn from each experience to improve your future efforts.

Embracing the Lessons of Heffalumps and Woozles

The Heffalumps and Woozles in Winnie the Pooh's dream represent the imaginary fears and distractions we face in our own lives. By understanding their true nature, that they are often more frightening in our minds than they are in real life, we can stop them from taking over our thoughts and actions. This helps us stay focused on our goals and move forward with confidence, clarity, and resilience.

The main point is that the fears and distractions that seem so overwhelming are often no more real than the Heffalumps and Woozles themselves. By confronting these imaginary enemies directly or simply setting them aside, you can create a life filled with purpose, joy, and fulfillment. Learn from Pooh and his friends, and let go of the imaginary barriers that hold you back. When you do this, you'll find that the way to your dreams becomes clearer and more achievable, allowing you to live a life without unnecessary fears and full of possibilities.

THE ART OF DOING NOTHING

93

The Wisdom of Doing Nothing

One lazy afternoon in the Hundred Acre Wood, Christopher Robin and Winnie the Pooh found themselves lounging beneath a big oak tree. The sun was warm, casting dappled shadows on the grass, and a soft breeze stirred the leaves above. Pooh lay on his back, gazing up at the sky, watching the clouds drift lazily by. Christopher Robin sat beside him, content in the stillness of the moment.

"*What are you doing, Christopher Robin?*" Pooh asked, puzzled by the quiet.

"*Nothing,*" replied Christopher Robin with a peaceful smile. "*What I like best is just doing nothing.*"

"*But what does 'doing nothing' mean?*" Pooh wondered aloud.

"*It's when someone asks you what you're going to do, and you say, 'nothing,'*" Christopher Robin explained, "*and then you actually do it. It means just being, Pooh—just enjoying the moment, without any plans or distractions.*"

Pooh nodded, letting the simple idea sink in. Together, they continued to do "nothing," and in that nothingness, they found everything they needed—a deep sense of peace, connection, and contentment.

The Noise of the Modern World

In today's world, the idea of "doing nothing" can seem almost radical. We live in an age of constant connectivity, where our attention is continually pulled in countless directions. The relentless barrage of notifications, messages, emails, and social media updates creates a constant state of mental stimulation that can leave us feeling exhausted and overwhelmed. The pressure to always be "on" and productive often makes us feel that doing nothing is a waste of time, when in reality, it can be one of the most valuable things we can do for our well-being.

Consider These Realities

- **Information Overload.** The average person is exposed to between 4,000 to 10,000 advertisements each day, including TV commercials, online ads, and brand messages (Forbes). This constant exposure leaves little room for mental rest.

- **Phone Dependence.** On average, we check our phones approximately 96 times per day, or about once every 10 minutes, making us feel like we are perpetually "on call" (Asurion, 2019).

- **Email Flood.** Over 300 billion emails are sent daily worldwide (Statista). The sheer volume of communication demands that we process and respond continuously, adding to our mental fatigue.

- **Social Media Saturation.** The typical social media user encounters around 285 pieces of content daily, including posts, ads, and stories from friends (Media Dynamics, 2021). This constant engagement leads to mental clutter and reduces our ability to focus deeply.

- **Media Consumption.** The average American adult spends over 11 hours a day consuming media—whether through TV, radio, internet, or apps (Nielsen, 2020). This habitual media consumption increases the "noise" in our lives, leaving little space for quiet reflection.

This overwhelming influx of information and distractions highlights the need for intentional breaks and moments of stillness. In our pursuit of constant productivity, we have lost the art of simply "being." But there is immense value in stepping back, doing nothing, and allowing ourselves to recharge.

Why We Struggle to Do Nothing

Modern culture glorifies busyness and productivity, often equating them with success and self-worth. As a result, many people feel guilty when they take time to relax or step away from their to-do lists. The pressure to always be "doing" something can make the concept of doing nothing feel unproductive or even indulgent. However, this mindset overlooks a fundamental truth: rest and relaxation are not the opposite of productivity; they are essential to it.

Imagine your typical weekday, packed with back-to-back meetings, emails, and a constant stream of notifications. You're always busy, proud of your ability to multitask, yet you often end the day feeling drained. Now, picture a weekend where you decide to unplug entirely. You turn off your phone, close your laptop, and retreat to a quiet cabin in the woods. At first, you feel restless and anxious, uncomfortable without the usual distractions. But as the hours pass, you start to relax. You go for a walk in the forest, read a book, or simply sit by the window, watching the world go by. By the end of the weekend, you feel deeply recharged. You realize that in doing nothing, you've allowed your mind to rest, your stress to dissipate, and your energy to return.

The Power of Mindfulness: Finding Presence in Doing Nothing

Mindfulness is the practice of being fully present in the moment and can help us embrace the art of doing nothing. Mindfulness is about stepping back from the hustle and bustle of life to find calm amid the chaos. Like Christopher Robin and Pooh lying under the oak tree, mindfulness is about appreciating the simplicity of just being and letting go of the need to constantly "do."

Steve Jobs, co-founder of Apple, was a strong advocate for mindfulness and meditation. Despite leading one of the world's most innovative companies, Jobs made time for meditation and stillness. He believed these practices were crucial for fostering creativity and mental clarity. In his biography, Jobs noted that meditation helped him see the value of simplicity and focus—two key principles that guided Apple's design philosophy.

In today's fast-paced world, we often run on fumes, relying on caffeine and sheer willpower to get through the day. When we think of "rest," most people automatically assume it means sleep. While sleep is crucial, it's only one type of rest, and focusing solely on physical rest may leave you feeling like you're never fully restored. In reality, there are seven distinct types of rest, each addressing different aspects of your well-being. In this article, we will explore these various kinds of rest and explain why each one is essential to living a balanced and rejuvenated life.

Physical Rest: More Than Just Sleep

Physical rest is the most obvious type of rest, and it includes both passive and active forms.

To Incorporate Physical Rest

- **Passive Physical Rest.** This involves sleep and napping, the core ways your body recharges itself. When you sleep, your body repairs tissues, grows muscles, and releases hormones that regulate stress, growth, and energy use. Most people know they need seven to nine hours of sleep per night to function optimally, but even if you hit that mark, you might still feel fatigued if you're missing out on other forms of rest.

- **Active Physical Rest.** This refers to engaging in low-impact activities like stretching, yoga, or walking. These activities help improve circulation, relieve muscle tension, and even boost energy levels. While it might seem counterintuitive, engaging in light movement can help your body rest more effectively than being completely sedentary. Physical rest, both passive and active, is essential to allow your body to recharge, but it's only the tip of the iceberg when it comes to holistic rejuvenation.

Mental Rest: Clearing the Clutter in Your Brain

Have you ever finished a full night of sleep only to wake up feeling mentally exhausted? That's a sign you may need mental rest. Mental fatigue comes from overthinking, multitasking, and absorbing too much information throughout the day. Whether you're constantly answering emails, attending meetings, or navigating life's never-ending to-do list, your brain is running at full capacity for much of the day.

To Incorporate Mental Rest Into Your Life, Try These Techniques

- **Take Breaks.** Schedule regular breaks during the day to stop and clear your head. Even just five minutes of breathing exercises or a short walk can work wonders.

- **Avoid Multitasking.** Focus on one task at a time to reduce cognitive overload. Multitasking might seem productive, but it often leads to decreased efficiency and increased mental fatigue.

- **Practice Mindfulness.** Mindfulness practices like meditation, deep breathing, or journaling help clear mental clutter and restore focus.

By giving your mind a chance to reset, you can come back to your work with renewed concentration and clarity.

Emotional Rest: Freeing Yourself from the Weight of Others' Expectations

Emotional rest is about feeling free to express your emotions without constantly managing how others perceive you. Many people find themselves navigating complicated relationships—whether personal or professional—where they have to suppress their feelings to avoid conflict or maintain a facade. Over time, this can lead to emotional exhaustion.

To Achieve Emotional Rest

- **Be Authentic.** Try to express your true feelings without fear of judgment. Emotional rest often comes when you stop pretending and start showing up as your authentic self.

- **Set Boundaries.** It's important to say "no" when needed and to create space between yourself and people or situations that drain you emotionally.

- **Seek Support.** Having a trusted confidant, whether a friend, family member, or therapist, can provide you with a safe space to release built-up emotions.

Emotional rest allows you to release pent-up feelings, preventing burnout and fostering healthier relationships.

Spiritual Rest: Reconnecting with Your Sense of Purpose

Spiritual rest is the kind of rest that goes beyond the physical and mental and taps into your sense of purpose and belonging. It's about feeling connected to something greater than yourself, whether through faith, community, nature, or meditation. A lack of spiritual rest may leave you feeling disconnected, unfulfilled, or questioning the meaning of life.

To Find Spiritual Rest

- **Engage in Reflection.** Spend time in quiet reflection, prayer, or meditation. This can help you reconnect with your core values and beliefs.

- **Give Back.** Volunteer work or helping others can offer a deep sense of fulfillment and provide a break from focusing solely on yourself.

- **Spend Time in Nature**. Many people find a spiritual connection when immersed in nature. Whether it's a walk in the woods or sitting by the ocean, the serenity of nature often fosters a sense of peace and purpose.

Spiritual rest can help you feel grounded and restore a sense of meaning and connection in your life.

Social Rest: Taking a Break from People Who Drain You

Social rest is often overlooked but is incredibly important, especially in our highly connected world. It's the kind of rest you need when you're constantly surrounded by people who drain your energy, whether intentionally or unintentionally. Social rest doesn't necessarily mean isolating yourself; instead, it's about being mindful of the company you keep.

To Achieve Social Rest

- **Identify Draining Relationships**. Recognize which relationships leave you feeling emotionally exhausted and which ones rejuvenate you. Spend more time with the latter and less with the former.

- **Balance Your Social Calendar**. Make room for quality time with those who uplift and energize you. Don't feel guilty for skipping out on social engagements that feel like an obligation.

- **Enjoy Solitude**. Sometimes the best way to rest socially is by enjoying time alone. This can help you reset and prepare for future interactions with others.

Social rest ensures you aren't constantly depleted by the energy of others and helps you maintain balance in your relationships.

Sensory Rest: Turning Down the Noise in a Distracting World

From the constant hum of technology to the flashing lights of our screens, modern life is full of sensory overload. Sensory rest is about giving your senses a break from this overstimulation, which can lead to stress and fatigue over time. Whether it's the blue light from screens, loud noises, or the sheer volume of information we consume daily, our senses are often overwhelmed.

To Restore Sensory Balance

- **Take Technology Breaks**. Set aside specific times during the day to unplug from your devices. This can be especially helpful before bed to promote better sleep.

- **Reduce Background Noise**. Find quiet spaces to relax, away from loud environments like busy offices or crowded public places.

- **Dim the Lights**. Opt for natural lighting when possible, and reduce your exposure to artificial lighting, especially before bedtime.

Giving your senses a chance to rest can help reduce stress and prevent sensory overload, allowing you to feel more centered and calm.

Creative Rest: Recharging Your Inspiration

Creative rest is particularly important for anyone in a creative field or those who constantly problem-solve and innovate. Even if you're not an artist, chances are you use creativity in your daily life—whether it's finding new ways to tackle challenges at work, brainstorming new ideas, or solving problems.

Creative rest is about rejuvenating your imagination and getting back in touch with inspiration. This might involve surrounding yourself with beauty, whether through art, music, nature, or new experiences. When you're creatively drained, the best thing you can do is step away from the problem and give your mind the freedom to wander.

To Experience Creative Rest

- **Immerse Yourself in Nature**. Spending time outdoors can help you reconnect with a sense of wonder and renewal, stimulating fresh ideas.

- **Engage With Art**. Visit an art gallery, watch a film, or listen to music that inspires you. Consuming the creative work of others can reignite your own creativity.

- **Take Breaks From Problem-Solving**. Step away from tasks that require creative thinking. Often, the best ideas come when you aren't actively trying to solve the problem.

Creative rest allows your mind to replenish itself, helping you return to your work with a fresh perspective.

Embracing a Holistic Approach to Rest

Rest is not just about sleep, and burnout is not just physical. To truly feel rested, you need to address all aspects of your well-being—physical, mental, emotional, spiritual, social, sensory, and creative. By recognizing the different kinds of rest and incorporating them into your routine, you can restore balance, prevent burnout, and live a more fulfilling and energized life.

The next time you feel tired, ask yourself: What kind of rest do I really need? Identifying the type of rest you're missing could be the key to unlocking greater productivity, peace, and well-being.

Practical Steps to Embrace the Art of Doing Nothing

- **Unplug Regularly**. Schedule time each day to disconnect from your devices. Even a brief break of 15-30 minutes without screens can refresh your mind. Consider turning off notifications during meals or designated "quiet hours" to reduce distractions.

- **Practice Mindfulness**. Engage in mindfulness exercises such as meditation, deep breathing, or simply observing your surroundings. You don't need to set aside hours for this—just a few moments of mindful awareness can help you reconnect with the present.

- **Take Nature Breaks**. Spend time outdoors, whether it's walking in the park, hiking in the woods, or sitting by a lake. Being in nature has been shown to lower stress levels, reduce anxiety, and promote feelings of well-being.

- **Schedule Downtime**. Treat downtime as a non-negotiable part of your daily or weekly routine. Block out time on your calendar for rest, just as you would for an important meeting. Whether it's a lazy Sunday morning or a quiet evening, prioritize moments of "nothingness."

- **Simplify Your Life**. Reduce clutter, both physical and mental. Let go of activities, commitments, or possessions that do not bring value or joy. The less cluttered your life is, the easier it becomes to find moments of stillness.

- **Embrace the "Slow Living" Movement**. Slow living is about doing things at a more leisurely pace and finding joy in the process rather than rushing to complete tasks. Whether it's enjoying your morning coffee without multitasking or taking a slow walk without checking your phone, these practices can bring a sense of calm and fulfillment.

The Benefits of Doing Nothing

The benefits of taking time to do nothing go beyond just feeling relaxed. Scientific research supports the idea that regular downtime can improve mental and physical health, enhance creativity, and even boost productivity. Here's how:

- **Enhances Creativity.** When we allow our minds to rest, we enter a state known as the "default mode network" (DMN) in the brain. This state is linked to creative thinking and problem-solving. Many people report experiencing "aha!" moments when their minds are at rest—like during a shower, a walk, or while daydreaming.

- **Improves Mental Health.** Regularly unplugging from the constant flow of information can help lower levels of cortisol, the stress hormone. By giving our brains a break, we can reduce anxiety, improve mood, and increase overall feelings of well-being.

- **Supports Memory Consolidation.** The brain needs rest to process and organize the information we take in daily. Studies have shown that periods of quiet reflection or "doing nothing" can aid in memory consolidation and learning retention.

- **Strengthens Relationships.** When we unplug and practice being present, we become more engaged in our relationships. This intentional presence allows us to listen more deeply and connect more meaningfully with those around us.

- **Boosts Productivity.** Ironically, taking breaks and allowing for downtime can lead to higher productivity. Studies have found that the brain can focus better and work more efficiently when it has had a chance to rest.

Embracing the Art of Doing Nothing in a Fast-Paced World

At the heart of Christopher Robin's wisdom is the understanding that sometimes, the best thing we can do is nothing at all. By doing nothing, we create space for rest, reflection, and renewal. In these moments of stillness, we find clarity, a sense of purpose, and a deeper connection to ourselves and the world around us. Imagine a world where we all took a little more time to simply be—pausing to appreciate the moments of our lives without rushing from one task to the next. By slowing down and allowing ourselves to do nothing, we may discover that these seemingly unproductive moments are, in fact, the most meaningful.

Finding Your Own Oak Tree

The next time you feel overwhelmed by the chaos of daily life, remember the simple wisdom of Christopher Robin. Embrace the art of doing nothing. Unplug, unwind, and just be. You might be surprised by how much you gain in moments of nothingness—whether it's a fresh perspective, a creative idea, or a sense of peace that had been missing.

Winnie the Pooh and his friends in the Hundred Acre Wood remind us that life doesn't have to be a constant rush from one activity to the next. There is profound beauty in slowing down, appreciating the present, and taking the time to do nothing. In embracing this simple lesson, we can find greater peace, clarity, and joy in our everyday lives.

So, go ahead—find your own oak tree, lie back, and let yourself do nothing. It just might turn out to be the best thing you do all day.

THE ART OF MINDSET REFRAMING

"It's not what we have, but what we enjoy that makes happiness."

A.A. Milne

Winnie the Pooh and his friends remind us that joy isn't found in possessions or circumstances—it's found in how we approach life. One day in the Hundred Acre Wood, the forest was filled with the warm glow of the setting sun, and everyone seemed busy with their usual routines. Piglet had been working on collecting acorns, Eeyore was searching for his lost tail (again), and Tigger had been bouncing here, there, and everywhere.

As Pooh wandered by, humming his usual happy tune, Piglet paused and said, "Pooh, you don't seem to have much today—no pot of honey, no grand plans—yet you look so very happy. How do you do it?"

Pooh smiled and replied, "It's not what we have, but what we enjoy that makes happiness, Piglet. I've got this lovely tune to hum, the warm sun on my nose, and you to chat with. That's quite enough for me to feel happy."

Inspired by Pooh's outlook, Piglet stopped worrying about collecting every last acorn, Tigger slowed down enough to notice the golden light in the trees, and even Eeyore stopped for a moment to enjoy the soft grass under his feet. By the end of the day, they realized that happiness had been with them all along—it was simply a matter of noticing and savoring the little joys of the moment.

In the art of mindset reframing, Pooh reminds us that the key to happiness lies not in waiting for everything to be perfect, but in appreciating what's already around us. It's about enjoying life as it comes, one honey pot—or one lovely moment—at a time.

Mindset Reframing

Pooh's simple but wise words, *"It never hurts to keep looking for sunshine,"* perfectly capture the idea of changing how we think about things. This practice, known as cognitive reframing in psychology, helps us see situations in a more positive or helpful way. It's about focusing on how we think, rather than what we think, and it's a powerful tool for boosting mental health and well-being.

The Science Behind Cognitive Reframing

- **Neuroplasticity**. Our brains are incredibly adaptable. Neuroplasticity refers to the brain's ability to reorganize itself by forming new connections. This means we can intentionally train our brains to respond more positively to situations.

- **Reduced Stress**. Research shows that cognitive reframing can significantly lower stress. By changing how we view stressors, we can lessen their impact on both our mental and physical health.

- **Better Mental Health**. Cognitive reframing is linked to improved mental health, including reduced anxiety and depression.

- **Better Problem-Solving**. Looking at problems from a different perspective can help us find more effective solutions.

- **Greater Resilienc**e. Reframing helps build resilience, making it easier for us to recover from setbacks.

6 Steps to Reframe Your Mindset

- **All-or-Nothing Thinking**. Seeing things as either all good or all bad. For example, "If I'm not completely successful, I'm a total failure."

- **Overgeneralization**. Making broad assumptions based on one event. For example, "I always mess things up."

- **Catastrophizing**. Expecting the worst possible outcome. For example, "If I make a mistake, everyone will think I'm incompetent."

- **Gather EvidenceCatastrophizing** This technique involves gathering evidence for and against your negative thoughts to see if they're really true. Start by writing down the thought you want to challenge, then list evidence that supports it and evidence that goes against it. If you think, "I'm terrible at my job," list your accomplishments and positive feedback as evidence that contradicts this thought. This can help you realize that your negative thinking isn't completely accurate.

- **Reframe**. Reframing means changing how you see a situation or thought to make it more positive or realistic. When a negative thought comes up, consciously turn it into a positive or neutral one. Instead of thinking, "I failed at this task," reframe it to, "This was a learning experience, and I can do better next time." This shift in perspective can lessen the emotional weight of the thought.

- **Thought Journaling**. Writing down your thoughts helps you analyze and understand them better. Keep a journal where you record your negative thoughts, the situations that triggered them, your emotional responses, and more balanced, alternative thoughts. If something stressful happens at work, write down your initial thoughts and feelings, then reframe them into something more positive. Reviewing your journal regularly can help you spot patterns and track your progress.

- **Socratic Questioning**. This method involves asking yourself questions to challenge and reframe negative thoughts. When faced with a negative thought, ask yourself:

- What evidence supports this thought?

- What evidence goes against it?

- Is this thought based on facts or feelings?

- What would I tell a friend who had this thought?

- How will I feel about this in a week or a month?

If you think, "I'm not good enough," ask yourself what evidence there is for and against it. Think about how you would advise a friend with the same thought. This can help you see things more clearly and fairly..

- **Positive Reinterpretation**. This involves finding a positive angle or lesson in a negative experience or thought. When something negative happens, ask yourself, "What can I learn from this?" or "Is there anything positive in this situation?" If you think, "I made a mistake at work," reframe it as, "This mistake taught me a valuable lesson and will help me improve in the future." This approach turns setbacks into opportunities for growth.

Examples of Mindset Reframing

Mindset reframing isn't just a theory. We see real-world examples of it everywhere.

- **Thomas Edison.** A famous inventor, he had an optimistic view of failure. When asked about the thousands of attempts it took to invent the light bulb, he said, "I have not failed. I've just found 10,000 ways that won't work." This is a perfect example of cognitive reframing. Instead of seeing each attempt as a failure, Edison saw them as necessary steps toward success. His ability to reframe challenges as learning experiences was key to his eventual achievements.

- **Nelson Mandela.** He spent 27 years in prison, but instead of letting it embitter him, he used that time to reflect, learn, and shape his vision for a free South Africa. Mandela's ability to view his imprisonment as a period of growth, rather than wasted time, shows the power of a positive mindset. His perspective helped him emerge from prison ready to lead his country toward reconciliation and democracy.

- **Oprah Winfrey**. A media mogul and philanthropist, she faced many challenges early in life, including poverty and abuse. But she didn't let these experiences define her. Instead, she reframed them as motivation to succeed and help others. Oprah's ability to turn struggles into strengths shows the power of reframing.

She often talks about the importance of seeing every experience as a lesson and using it to grow.

Practical Exercises for Mindset Reframing

- **Daily Gratitude Practice**. Start each day by writing down three things you're grateful for. This helps shift your focus from what's missing to what's already abundant in your life.

- **Mindfulness Meditation**. Spend a few minutes each day practicing mindfulness. Focus on your breathing and observe your thoughts without judgment. This helps you become more aware of your thought patterns and more capable of reframing negative ones.

- **Reframing Challenge**. Pick one negative thought each day and consciously reframe it. Write down the original thought and your new, positive perspective. Over time, this practice can train your brain to naturally adopt a more positive outlook.

- **Visualization**. Imagine a challenging situation and picture yourself handling it successfully. This reduces anxiety and builds confidence, making it easier to approach real-life situations with a positive mindset.

Cognitive reframing is a powerful way to change how we experience the world. By shifting our perspective, we can lower stress, improve mental health, and boost our overall well-being. Winnie the Pooh's wisdom, "It never hurts to keep looking for sunshine," reminds us that our mindset shapes our reality. By adopting a positive outlook and practicing cognitive reframing, we can find joy and fulfillment, even during tough times.

Remember, how we view our experiences can turn a rainy day into an adventure, a failure into a lesson, and a setback into a stepping stone. So, like Pooh, keep looking for sunshine and discover the beauty and potential in every moment.

SIMPLICITY IN CHAOS

"TTFN! Ta-ta for now!"

Tigger

With his boundless energy, unshakable optimism, and lively bounces, Tigger is more than just the spirited character of the Hundred Acre Wood—he's a symbol of living with clarity and purpose, even when life feels chaotic. While his carefree attitude might give the impression that he doesn't take things seriously, Tigger's approach actually holds deep wisdom. He shows us how to cut through distractions, face life's challenges head-on, and find simplicity amidst the complexity. His famous phrases like "Don't be ridikkerous!" serve as reminders to focus on what truly matters, embrace straightforward thinking, and move forward with confidence, no matter what obstacles lie ahead.

In a world where we are constantly bombarded with information, choices, and competing demands, it's easy to feel overwhelmed and lose sight of our goals. Tigger's lighthearted yet purposeful approach encourages us to take a step back, simplify our thoughts, and find clarity in the midst of life's hustle and bustle. His unique way of handling uncertainty and challenges can teach us valuable lessons about decision-making, focus, resilience, and embracing simplicity.

Diving into Tigger's timeless wisdom and exploring, helps us to learn how we can apply it to our own lives, from navigating professional hurdles to achieving personal growth. Whether you're facing a tough decision at work, juggling multiple responsibilities, or struggling to find balance, Tigger's lively spirit can guide you to approach every situation with clear goals, bold action, and a bounce in your step. As we'll see, finding clarity amidst chaos isn't just about surviving—it's about thriving with enthusiasm and joy.

Insight No. 1 — Simplifying Decision-Making in Professional Settings

- **Tigger's Insight**. Tigger doesn't waste time overthinking or doubting himself. He knows what he wants and goes after it with confidence, cutting through distractions to focus on what's important.

- **Application in the Workplace**. In professional settings, decision-making can often become complicated and drawn out due to over-analysis and too many opinions. Tigger's approach reminds us of the value of simplicity in decision-making. By focusing on clear goals and avoiding unnecessary complications, we can make more effective and timely decisions. Imagine you're leading a project with multiple stakeholders, each with different opinions. Instead of getting overwhelmed by the differing perspectives, follow Tigger's lead: focus on the core objectives and make decisions that align with those goals. This helps streamline the decision-making process, reduces delays, and keeps the project on track.

- **Practical Steps.**

  - **Clarify Objectives**. Begin by clearly stating the goals of your project or task. What is the main result you want to reach?

- **Avoid Over-Complication**. When you have several options, remove the ones that don't directly help you achieve your main goals.

- **Trust Your Judgment**. After making a decision, stick to it with confidence and avoid doubting yourself unless new information changes things.

Insight No. 2 — Maintaining Focus Amidst Personal Life's Chaos

- **Tigger's Insight**. Even with chaos around him, Tigger stays focused on his goals. He knows what he wants, whether it's bouncing higher or reaching something bigger, and doesn't let distractions stop him.

- **Application in Personal Life.** In our daily lives, distractions are everywhere, social media, never-ending to-do lists, and constant notifications. Tigger's focus amid the chaos teaches us an important lesson about staying clear and purposeful in our own efforts. If you're working on a personal goal like learning a new skill or improving your health, it's easy to get distracted by everyday demands. Tigger's approach reminds us to stay determined and focused, even when distractions are everywhere. Make a clear plan for reaching your goal and stick to it, making sure your daily actions match your long-term goals.

- **Practical Steps.**

  - **Set Clear Goals**. Clearly define what you want to achieve and break it down into small, manageable steps.

  - **Eliminate Distractions**. Identify what usually distracts you from your goals and find ways to reduce or avoid them.

  - **Stay Committed.** Regularly remind yourself why your goals matter. Keep your focus strong by checking your progress and making adjustments as needed.

Insight No. 3 — Facing Brutal Truths with Courage

- **Tigger's Insight**. Tigger isn't afraid to face the truth. He knows it's important to confront the hard realities of any situation and respond accordingly.

- **Application in Personal and Professional Growth**. Facing hard truths can be uncomfortable, whether at work or in our personal lives. It means recognizing where we may be falling short or understanding the challenges ahead. Tigger's wisdom teaches us that by facing these truths directly, we can better manage life's challenges and make informed choices that lead to growth and success. If you're in a job where you're not meeting your own or others' expectations, it might be tempting to ignore the problem or make excuses. However, by following Tigger's approach and facing the truth perhaps by seeking feedback or reevaluating your plan you can take practical steps to improve and overcome challenges.

- **Practical Steps.**

  - ○ **Conduct Honest Self-Assessment**. Regularly review your progress and performance in both personal and work settings. Find areas where you can improve.

  - ○ **Seek Constructive Feedback**. Don't avoid feedback, even if it's hard to hear. Use it to help you grow and improve.

  - ○ **Take Decisive Action**: After identifying the hard truths, make a plan to tackle them and take action right away. Don't let fear or discomfort stop you.

Insight No. 4 — Moving Forward with Confidence and Determination

- **Tigger's Insight**. Tigger is known for his strong confidence and determination. When he focuses on a goal, he leaps forward with energy and determination, ready to face any challenge.

- **Application in Overcoming Challenges**. Confidence and determination are essential when facing challenges, whether in your career or personal life. Tigger's approach shows us the importance of believing in ourselves and moving forward with purpose, even when the way ahead is unclear. If you're facing a big challenge, like starting a new business or making a major life change, doubt and fear can easily creep in. However, by embracing Tigger's confidence, you can overcome these challenges with determination. Focus on your strengths, trust in your abilities, and take bold steps toward your goals, knowing that resilience and perseverance will help you succeed.

- **Practical Steps.**

  - ○ **Cultivate Self-Belief**. Keep reminding yourself of your past achievements and the skills you've gained. Use these to help boost your confidence.

  - ○ **Set Bold Goals**. Don't hesitate to dream big. Set challenging goals and break them into smaller, manageable steps.

○ **Embrace Challenges**. See challenges as chances to grow instead of roadblocks. Tackle them with the same energy and determination that Tigger has when he bounces.

Insight No. 5 — Embracing Simplicity and Clarity in All Aspects of Life

- **Tigger's Insight**. Simplicity is central to Tigger's way of thinking. By cutting out the distractions and focusing on what really matters, he can live with clear goals and purpose.

- **Application in Achieving Life Balance**. In a world full of complexities and constant demands, it's easy to forget what really matters. Tigger's wisdom reminds us to simplify our lives by focusing on the essentials like our goals, relationships, and well-being. If you're feeling overwhelmed by everything asking for your time, it might be time to rethink your priorities. Use Tigger's principle of simplicity to identify what's most important in your life and cut out distractions that don't help these priorities. This can lead to a more balanced and fulfilling life, allowing you to focus your energy on what truly counts.

- **Practical Steps.**

  ○ **Identify Core Priorities**. Think about what matters most to you, whether it's your job, family, health, or personal growth. Focus on these key areas.

  ○ **Simplify Your Routine**. Get rid of tasks or commitments that don't match your main priorities. Make your daily routine simpler to lower stress and gain clarity.

  ○ **Live with Intention**. Make choices that align with your values and goals. Try not to get lost in the chaos of everyday life.

Bouncing Toward Success with Tigger's Wisdom

Tigger's wisdom, shown through his lively personality and simple catchphrases, offers important lessons for dealing with the chaos of modern life. Whether at work or in personal goals, Tigger teaches us the value of clarity, confidence, and simplicity. By following these ideas, we can cut through the noise, focus on what truly matters, and move forward with purpose and determination.

As you face life's challenges and opportunities, remember to tap into your inner Tigger. Embrace clarity in the chaos, face tough truths with bravery, and bounce toward your goals with confidence and energy. By doing this, you'll discover that the path to success is not only possible but also filled with joy and fulfillment.

POOH'S WISDOM – AVOIDING COMPLEXITY

"Sometimes the smallest things take up the most room in your heart."

A.A. Milne

In the Hundred Acre Wood, life was rarely grand or extravagant, yet it was always full of meaning. Pooh and his friends didn't have castles or riches; they didn't chase after the big or the flashy. Instead, they found joy in the tiniest moments—a shared pot of honey, a walk through the forest, or the simple pleasure of being together. Pooh, with his gentle and unassuming wisdom, knew better than most that it's not the size of a thing that matters, but the space it occupies in your heart.

Today, in a world that often pushes us to strive for more—more achievements, more possessions, more complexity—it's easy to overlook the power of small, meaningful moments. Pooh's way of thinking reminds us to slow down, to savor the seemingly ordinary, and to recognize that true happiness often lives in the little things: a kind word, a quiet sunrise, a moment of connection with a loved one.

Pooh's ability to find joy in the simplest parts of life is a testament to his timeless wisdom. It's not about ignoring challenges or ambitions; it's about anchoring ourselves in gratitude and remembering that the smallest things—a thoughtful gesture, a cherished memory, or the warmth of a friend—can bring the greatest happiness.

As we explore Pooh's insights, we'll see how his approach to life encourages us to focus on what truly matters. By appreciating the small joys and allowing them to fill our hearts, we can find clarity, balance, and fulfillment in a world that often feels overwhelming. So, let's take a moment to embrace Pooh's wisdom, treasure the smallest things, and make room for what matters most.

Insight No. 1 — The Power of Simplicity in Professional Decision-Making

- **Pooh's Insight.** Pooh doesn't pretend to know more than he does. He tackles challenges with a simple approach, valuing straightforwardness over complexity.

- **Application in the Workplace.** In professional settings, experts often feel the need to show their intelligence by overthinking and complicating decisions. Pooh's wisdom offers a different path embracing simplicity. By cutting through the noise and focusing on the main issue, we can make better decisions. When leading a team meeting, instead of getting stuck in technical jargon or too much data, try Pooh's method: focus on the basic goals and ask simple, clear questions. This approach can lead to more productive discussions and quicker solutions.

- **Practical Steps.**

  - **Ask Basic Questions**. Begin with the most basic questions. What is the problem we need to solve? What are the key steps to take?

  - **Avoid Unnecessary Complexity**. If solutions start to feel too complicated, take a step back and look for simpler options that can achieve the same goal.

- ○ **Encourage Open Dialogue**. Create a space where team members feel safe sharing ideas without fear of being judged, just as Pooh listens to his friends' suggestions without bias.

Insight No. 2 — Maintaining Humility and Curiosity in Personal Growth

- **Pooh's Insight.** Pooh's humble nature and curiosity help him learn from every experience. He approaches each situation with an open mind, ready to gain new insights.

- **Application in Personal Life.** In our personal lives, it's easy to become defensive or closed off when facing challenges. Pooh's way teaches us the value of humility and curiosity. By admitting what we don't know and being open to learning, we can grow and find clarity in situations that might feel overwhelming. If you're trying to learn a new skill or understand a complicated issue, embrace your innocence like Pooh. Instead of pretending to know more than you do, ask questions and look for simple explanations. This will help you build a strong foundation of knowledge.

- **Practical Steps.**

  - ○ **Stay Curious**. Always feel free to ask questions, even if they seem simple. Curiosity leads to a deeper understanding.

  - ○ **Embrace Humility**. Recognize when you don't know something. This openness encourages others to share their knowledge with you.

  - ○ **Learn Continuously**. Treat each day as a chance to learn something new, just as Pooh explores his world with fresh eyes.

Insight No. 3 — Overcoming Complexity by Returning to Basics

- **Pooh's Insight.** Pooh doesn't overthink. When things get complicated, he goes back to the basics, finding clarity in simplicity.

- **Application in Managing Overwhelm.** In today's fast-paced world, we often feel overwhelmed by too much information and too many choices. Pooh's method of cutting through complexity by focusing on the basics is a powerful way to manage overwhelm. By simplifying our approach, we can discover solutions that were hidden by unnecessary details. If you're feeling overwhelmed by a big project, take a step back and break it down into its simplest parts. Identify the main goals and focus on achieving them one step at a time.

- **Practical Steps.**

  - **Simplify Your Approach**. Break complex tasks into smaller, manageable steps that focus on the main goals.

  - **Cut Through the Noise**. Remove distractions and unnecessary details that make the issue more complicated.

  - **Revisit the Fundamentals**. When you're stuck, go back to the basics and rebuild your approach from the ground up.

Insight No. 4 — Avoiding the Pitfall of Overcomplication

- **Pooh's Insight.** Pooh knows that *"very smart people will often outsmart themselves"* by making simple matters too complicated. He prefers straightforward solutions.

- **Application in Problem-Solving.** Experts often fall into the trap of overcomplicating problems, which makes it harder to find a solution. Pooh's approach teaches us to avoid this by sticking to clear, simple solutions. If you're trying to solve a complex problem, resist the urge to add unnecessary layers of analysis. Instead, focus on the simplest and most direct path to a solution.

- **Practical Steps.**

  - **Keep It Simple**. Focus on the most direct solutions to problems, steering clear of unnecessary complexity.

  - **Trust Simplicity**. Believe in simple solutions, even if they seem too obvious.

  - **Reevaluate When Stuck**. If a solution isn't working, simplify it and start over.

Insight No. 5 — Simplicity as a Virtue in Professional and Personal Life

- **Pooh's Insight.** Pooh's view shows the power of simplicity. He reminds us that life's challenges often have simpler answers than we first think.

- **Application in Modern Life.** In a world full of complexity, the wisdom of simplicity shines as a clear guide. Great thinkers like Confucius and Leonardo da Vinci have praised simplicity as a virtue. Confucius said, *"Life is really simple, but we insist on making it complicated,"* while da Vinci stated, *"Simplicity is the ultimate sophistication."* These timeless insights remind us that true sophistication comes from removing the unnecessary to uncover the core essence of any topic. For instance, in the workplace, simplifying processes can lead to better efficiency and clarity. By focusing on the basic parts of a project and avoiding extra complications, you can accomplish more with less effort.

- **Practical Steps.**

    ◦ **Focus on Essentials**. Identify the key parts of any task or challenge and prioritize them.

    ◦ **Eliminate the Unnecessary**. Get rid of any extra steps or details that don't help you reach your main goal.

    ◦ **Practice Patience**. Like Pooh, be patient with yourself and others. Sometimes, seeing things clearly takes time.

Insight No. 6 — Mastering the Art of Knowing What to Overlook

- **Pooh's Insight.** Pooh's patience and simplicity echo William James's belief that "The art of being wise is the art of knowing what to overlook."

- **Application in Decision-Making.** In both personal and professional life, wisdom often means knowing what truly matters. This idea connects with the natural world, where simplicity usually leads the way. Isaac Newton noted, *"Nature is pleased with simplicity. And nature is no dummy."* Nature's complex designs are based on simple principles that create beautiful results. When faced with too much information or a tough decision, focus on the key factors that will lead to success. By simplifying your decision-making process, you can avoid feeling overwhelmed and make better choices.

- **Practical Steps.**

    ◦ **Prioritize Key Factors**. Focus on what will have the biggest impact on the outcome.

    ◦ **Practice Discernment**. Learn to identify which details are important and which can be ignored.

    ◦ **Trust in Simplicity**. Believe that the simplest approach often brings the best results.

Insight No. 7 — Simplicity in Expression and Communication

- **Pooh's Insight.** Just as Pooh's simple words hold deep wisdom, Walt Whitman and Coco Chanel recognized the power of simplicity in communication. Whitman said, *"Simplicity is the glory of expression,"* while Chanel stated, *"Simplicity is the keynote of all true elegance."*

- **Application in Communication.** In both business and personal relationships, clear and direct communication is essential. Albert Einstein advised, "Everything should be made as simple as possible, but not simpler." This principle highlights the need to find the most effective way to share your message without making it too simple.In a business presentation, aim to express your ideas clearly and directly. Avoid jargon and unnecessary details that could confuse your audience. Instead, focus on delivering your message in a way that is easy to understand and impactful.

- **Practical Steps.**

   - **Be Clear and Concise**. Deliver your message in the simplest and most direct way possible.

   - **Avoid Jargon**. Use plain language that everyone can understand, no matter their background.

   - **Edit Ruthlessly**. Cut out any unnecessary words or phrases that don't help make your message clear.

Insight No. 8 — Finding Profound Ideas in Simple Concepts

- **Pooh's Insight.** Pooh's ability to see things simply yet deeply reflects William Golding's observation that "The greatest ideas are the simplest."

- **Application in Innovation and Creativity.** The most impactful ideas often come from simple concepts. Henry David Thoreau encouraged us to *"Simplify, simplify."* In a world full of distractions and complexities, simplifying our approach can lead to greater clarity, purpose, and creativity. When brainstorming new ideas, start with a simple concept and build on it. Often, the most successful innovations are those that solve problems in a straightforward and easy-to-understand way.

- **Practical Steps.**

  - **Start Simple**. Begin with a basic idea and refine it until it becomes something strong.

  - **Avoid Over-Complication**. Resist the urge to add extra elements to your ideas.

  - **Focus on Clarity**. Make sure your ideas can be easily shared and understood by others.

Insight No. 9 — Embracing Simplicity in Everyday Life

- **Pooh's Insight.** Like Pooh, who finds joy in simple things, Paulo Coelho reminds us that *"The simple things are also the most extraordinary things, and only the wise can see them."*

- **Application in Daily Life.** Embracing simplicity in our daily routines can lead to greater fulfillment. Whether it's simplifying your schedule, decluttering your home, or focusing on what truly matters, simplicity helps us live more meaningful and balanced lives. If you're feeling overwhelmed by your daily responsibilities, take a step back and simplify your routine. Focus on what's most important and let go of tasks that don't help your well-being or goals.

- **Practical Steps.**

  - **Simplify Your Routine**. Focus on essential tasks and remove the unnecessary ones.

  - **Appreciate Simple Joys**. Take time to enjoy the small pleasures in life, like spending time with loved ones or appreciating nature.

  - **Live Intentionally**. Make choices that reflect your values and priorities, simplifying your life along the way.

Embracing Clarity Through Naivete

Winnie the Pooh's wisdom, grounded in his simplicity and humility, offers valuable lessons for dealing with the challenges of modern life. Whether at work or in personal situations, Pooh shows us the importance of being open-minded when facing difficulties by focusing on the basics. By following these ideas, we can cut through the clutter, gain clarity, and make choices that lead to success and satisfaction.

As you encounter life's challenges, remember to tap into your inner Pooh. Embrace simplicity, stay curious, and don't hesitate to ask simple questions. By doing this, you'll find the clarity and purpose needed to handle any situation with grace and wisdom.

EMBRACING PATIENCE IN LIFE'S JOURNEY

"Rivers know this: There is no hurry. We shall get there someday."

Winnie the Pooh

Pooh's metaphor of the river is a call to appreciate each moment, find strength in persistence, and cultivate the ability to adapt. It encourages us to embrace life's natural flow, understanding that true growth often requires time. Instead of fighting against the current or demanding immediate outcomes, we can learn to trust that, like the river, we'll reach our destination in time. Through this approach, we not only alleviate the pressure to constantly hurry but also find peace and contentment in the progress we make along the way.

The lessons from the river's journey can be applied to many aspects of life—from overcoming professional setbacks to finding calm in a world full of demands. Let's dive into how adopting a patient mindset, inspired by Pooh's wisdom, can help us face life's obstacles with resilience, find joy in the present, and embrace the steady progress that leads to true fulfillment. Just like rivers that move slowly but steadily through the land, we can also learn to be patient, trusting that we'll get where we need to be in time.

Insight No. 1 — The River as a Metaphor for Life's Journey

- **Pooh's Insight.** Pooh's comparison to the river perfectly shows the power of steady, purposeful progress. Just as rivers flow at their own pace, cutting through mountains, valleys, and plains, we too can move through life without rushing, trusting the natural flow of time.

- **Applying This in Modern Life.** In today's fast-paced world, patience is often overlooked. We're used to wanting instant results. But Pooh's wisdom encourages us to see things differently. The river's slow and steady path reminds us that there's value in taking our time. By moving carefully and mindfully, we can appreciate the journey and learn from it. For example, when working toward a long-term goal, instead of getting frustrated by how long it takes, we can adopt the river's mindset. Trusting the process allows us to focus on each step, knowing that we'll get to our destination in time.

- **Practical Steps.**

  - **Embrace Steady Progress.** Focus on making consistent efforts instead of rushing for quick results.

  - **Trust the Journey.** Believe that you will reach your goals in time, just like a river eventually flows to the sea.

  - **Practice Mindfulness.** Stay present in each moment of your journey, appreciating the process rather than focusing only on the end result.

Insight No. 2 — The Power of Persistence and Resilience

- **Pooh's Insight.** The river's journey shows persistence. It keeps flowing, finding ways around obstacles, just as we must navigate challenges in our own lives.

- **Application in Overcoming Obstacles.** The strength of the river is in its resilience and constant motion. As Albert Einstein said, *"Life is like riding a bicycle. To keep your balance, you must keep moving."* This emphasizes the need for continuous effort and persistence, like the river that never stops flowing. When you face setbacks in your career or personal life, think of the river's resilience. Instead of giving up, find a way around the obstacle and keep moving forward.

- **Practical Steps.**

  - **Keep Moving**. Even if progress is slow, keep taking steps toward your goals.

  - **Adapt to Challenges**. Like a river flowing around rocks, be flexible and find new ways when you face obstacles.

  - **Cultivate Resilience**. Strengthen your ability to keep going through tough times by staying focused on your long-term goals.

Insight No. 3 — The Value of Patience in a Fast-Paced World

- **Pooh's Insight.** Pooh's wisdom reminds us that patience isn't about being passive; it's about trusting the process. By moving steadily and mindfully, like a river, we can find calm and reassurance.

- **Application in Managing Modern Pressures.** In today's world, we are constantly bombarded with messages telling us to move faster and do more. This pressure can cause stress and burnout. However, by adopting the river's philosophy, we can find calm and trust that we will reach our goals, even if it takes time. When you feel overwhelmed by your job or personal responsibilities, take a step back and evaluate your pace. Let yourself slow down and trust that everything will unfold as it should.

- **Practical Steps.**

  - **Slow Down.** Resist the urge to rush through tasks. Take your time to do things right.

  - **Prioritize Well-Being**. Set aside time for rest and self-care, knowing that a slower pace can lead to greater long-term success.

- ○ **Trust in Timing**. Believe that the right opportunities and outcomes will come at the right time.

Insight No. 4 — Finding Peace in the Present Moment

- **Pooh's Insight.** The river, flowing gently and steadily, encourages us to slow down and appreciate the present moment. It teaches us that each moment is part of the journey and that every step we take has value.

- **Application in Everyday Life.** Looking at the river's journey, we see that patience isn't about being passive or inactive. It's about being present and appreciating the journey. By adopting this mindset, we can ease our anxiety and create a sense of peace and contentment. If you find yourself constantly worrying about future goals, take a moment to pause and enjoy your current surroundings. Embrace the process and the present moment, knowing that it's an important part of your journey.

- **Practical Steps.**

  - ○ **Be Present**. Focus on what is happening right now instead of constantly worrying about the future.

  - ○ **Appreciate the Journey**. Enjoy the small moments and milestones along the way.

  - ○ **Practice Gratitude**. Take time to reflect on what you are thankful for in the present, which helps keep you grounded in the moment.

Insight No. 5 — The Importance of Compassion and Self-Kindness

- **Pooh's Insight.** The river's journey reminds us to be kinder to ourselves. Just as the river flows at its own pace, we should give ourselves the time and grace to grow without self-judgment.

- **Application in Self-Compassion.** Often, we are our own toughest critics, setting unrealistic expectations and feeling frustrated when we don't meet them. By adopting the river's philosophy, we can learn to be more compassionate and forgiving toward ourselves. We can understand that growth takes time and that it's okay to move at our own pace. If you're struggling with personal growth or development, remember that progress isn't always a straight line. Give yourself the time to grow at your own speed without comparing yourself to others.

- **Practical Steps.**

    - **Be Gentle with Yourself**. Remember that it's okay to go at your own pace and that not all progress shows right away.

    - **Avoid Comparisons.** Concentrate on your own path instead of comparing yourself to others.

    - **Celebrate Small Wins**. Recognize and celebrate every step forward, no matter how tiny.

Embracing the Wisdom of Patience

Winnie the Pooh's quote about rivers and patience teaches us an important lesson for our lives. It reminds us that we don't need to rush and that we will reach our goals in time. By following the river's calm and steady way, we can find peace, keep going, and appreciate the journey more. As we face life's challenges, let's learn from rivers and embrace the wisdom of patience. By moving steadily, trusting the process, and being present in each moment, we will get there one day just like the river finds its way to the sea.

USE LANGUAGE THAT A 12 YEAR COULD UNDERSTAND

"It is more fun to talk with someone who doesn't use long, difficult words but rather short, easy words like, 'What about lunch?'

Winnie the Pooh

One sunny morning in the Hundred Acre Wood, Winnie the Pooh was enjoying his favorite pastime—sitting on a log with a jar of honey. As he savored the sweet taste, he noticed Piglet approaching with a concerned expression.

"Pooh," Piglet began, *"I just talked to Owl, and he used such big words that I got lost. I didn't understand a single thing he said."*

Pooh paused, honey dripping from his paw. *"Big words, you say? Oh dear, that doesn't sound very friendly at all,"* he replied. *"Why use big words when small ones are so much friendlier and easier to understand?"*

Piglet's face brightened with relief. *"Exactly, Pooh! Simple words are much better."*

Pooh gave a thoughtful nod, feeling the warmth of friendship fill the air. *"Well then, Piglet,"* he said, *"let's talk about something simple. How about... lunch?"*

Piglet's eyes lit up, and the two friends spent the rest of the afternoon chatting about their favorite foods—honey, acorns, and dandelion sandwiches. They laughed and shared stories, enjoying each other's company without ever needing to use long, complicated words. For Pooh and Piglet, the joy of friendship wasn't about impressing each other with fancy language; it was about sharing simple moments and speaking from the heart.

What Does the Research Say?

A recent study found that 84% of readers are put off by fancy language. These aren't just big words; they kill engagement! Ever wondered why a well-crafted post filled with polished phrases gets fewer likes than a simple one? It's not your content; it's the words you use. People aren't impressed, they're confused! Research shows that using jargon can hurt communication. Here are some key studies and their findings:

- **The Journal of Language and Social Psychology** (2008) found that using technical jargon made speakers seem less trustworthy and less likable. Participants rated those who used complex language as less intelligent compared to those who used simpler words. Too much jargon can make communicators seem less competent and approachable.

- **The Harvard Business Review** (2012) showed that business professionals who used plain language were more successful in getting their messages across. Jargon confused the audience and made them less likely to engage. Clear, simple language boosts audience engagement and helps them remember the message.

- An experiment by **Princeton University** (2005) showed that writers using complicated language were seen as less intelligent than those who used simple language, even when the content was the same. Using complex words unnecessarily can backfire and make communicators seem less smart.

- A study by **Applied Cognitive Psychology** (2012) found that jargon in teaching materials lowered understanding and learning. Students who read texts with jargon scored lower on comprehension tests than those who read plain language. Jargon can hinder learning, making it less effective for education.

- A survey by the **Nielsen Norman Group** (2011) revealed that websites with jargon-heavy content had higher bounce rates and less user engagement. Users often left quickly when faced with complicated language, preferring sites with clear information. In online communication, jargon leads to poor user experiences and lower engagement.

Big words can make your message convoluted, create distance with your audience, kill emotional connection, and make you seem less credible! Jargon isn't the 'secret sauce' to look smart; it's the 'poison pill' that kills interest. In today's busy world, we are overwhelmed with information, making it hard to find what's important. As a result, our messages are often misunderstood or ignored. What's the solution?

Simplify. Simplify. Simplify.

Elon Musk, the leader of SpaceX and Tesla, has a "no-jargon" policy in his companies. Musk believes that simplicity leads to clarity, efficiency, and innovation. His straightforward approach ensures that ideas are communicated well, which is vital when dealing with complex technology. In an interview, Musk said that any engineer who can't explain their work to a layperson doesn't understand it well enough. This focus on simplicity helps not only internal communication but also makes SpaceX's ambitious goals clearer and more exciting to the public.

Maya Angelou, a famous poet and civil rights activist, said, "People will forget what you said, people will forget what you did, but people will never forget how you made them feel." This quote highlights that the power of communication lies not in the words but in the feelings they create.

When we remove jargon and speak from the heart, we connect on a deeper level. Simple, clear language makes people feel valued and understood. It's not about dumbing down the message but making it accessible and relatable.

The Wisdom of Clear Communication

Using simple language doesn't mean limiting the depth of your ideas; it means making your ideas accessible to others. Look at Warren Buffett, one of the world's most successful investors, who is known for his plain-spoken manner. In his annual letters to shareholders, Buffett avoids jargon and complex financial terms. Instead, he uses everyday language to explain tough concepts in ways that anyone can grasp. His approach not only builds trust but also ensures that his message reaches a broad audience. He once said, *"If you can't explain it simply, you don't understand it well enough."* This reflects a key truth: clarity in communication is a sign of mastery, not weakness.

The lesson from Buffett, as well as from Pooh, is that effective communication isn't about showing off your vocabulary. It's about making sure your message is understood. By speaking plainly, you invite others to join the conversation. You create a space where ideas can be shared freely, without anyone feeling left out or confused. After all, language is meant to connect people, not create barriers.

Why Simplicity Matters

When we strip away unnecessary complexity, we make room for genuine connection. Words are powerful tools, but when they're used to impress rather than to communicate, they can lose their impact. Think about the last time you heard someone speak in a way that was overly complicated. Did you feel inspired, or did you find yourself struggling to follow along? Contrast that with a time when someone explained a difficult concept using simple, relatable language. The difference is clear: simplicity helps build understanding.

When Piglet and Pooh decided to talk about lunch instead of complicated topics, they were not just choosing an easy conversation—they were choosing connection. They understood that sharing simple joys, like honey and dandelion sandwiches, was more important than sounding clever. This principle applies to all our conversations, whether we're talking to a friend, giving a presentation, or writing an email. Simple language fosters an environment where everyone feels included and valued.

Applying Pooh's Wisdom in Everyday Communication

So how can we apply this lesson from Pooh, Piglet, and Warren Buffett to our daily lives? Here are some practical tips:

- **Know Your Audience.** Tailor your language to fit the people you're speaking to. Avoid jargon unless you're sure everyone understands it. If you're explaining something complex, break it down into simpler terms.

- **Be Clear and Concise.** Focus on the main points. Don't fill your message with extra words that can make it hard to follow. Remember, if you can explain it in fewer words, it's probably more effective.

- **Use Analogies and Stories.** Just as Pooh and Piglet talked about lunch, you can use everyday examples to illustrate more complicated ideas. Analogies make concepts relatable and memorable.

- **Ask for Feedback.** After explaining something, check if the other person understands. Invite questions and be willing to clarify if needed. This not only ensures comprehension but also shows that you care about the listener's experience.

The Joy of Simple Conversations

Imagine a world where business meetings and everyday conversations are as pleasant and straightforward as lunch with a friend. When we choose to use clear language, we aren't just making communication easier; we're making it more enjoyable. We're removing the barriers that jargon can create and inviting people to connect on a deeper level.

Pooh's wisdom about using *"short, easy words"* is not just about language—it's about valuing the person you're speaking to. It's about recognizing that the goal of communication is not to show off but to share, to understand, and to be understood. Whether you're giving a presentation, writing a report, or having a chat with a friend, remember that keeping it simple can make a world of difference.

Communication with Heart

In the end, what matters is not the size of the words we use but the size of the heart behind them. Winnie the Pooh may not have been an expert in business or linguistics, but his simple approach to communication offers a timeless lesson. By embracing simplicity and speaking in ways that everyone can understand, we create opportunities for connection, learning, and growth. So, the next time you find yourself tempted to impress with big words, take a page from Pooh's book and keep it friendly and simple.

After all, sometimes all it takes to bring people together is a simple question like, *"What about lunch?"* Let's follow Pooh's lead and remember that the best conversations are not about showing off how much we know, but about sharing the simple joys that connect us all.

THE WISDOM OF A BIG HEART

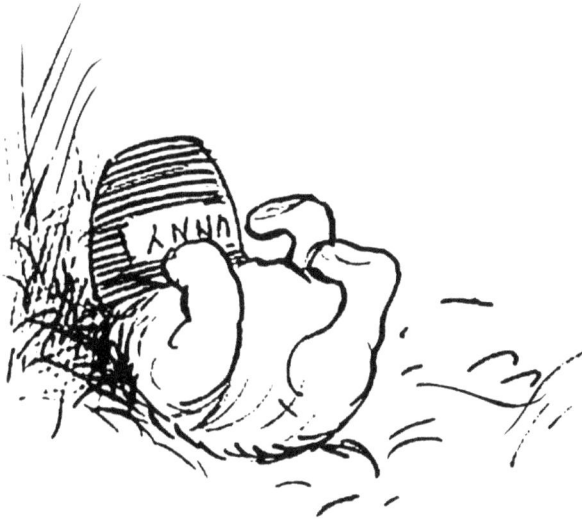

"Well, I am a bear of very little brain," said Pooh.
"No, Pooh. You are, I think, a bear of a very big heart," replied Christopher Robin.

The gentle exchange between Pooh and Christopher Robin captures a powerful message about the value of kindness, empathy, and emotional depth. While Pooh might doubt his intellect, Christopher Robin sees something far more valuable in his friend—a big heart. In today's world, we would call this quality Emotional Intelligence (EI) or Emotional Quotient (EQ). It represents an ability to understand and manage one's own emotions while also being sensitive to the emotions of others. Pooh's adventures may appear simple on the surface, but his ability to empathize, forgive, and support his friends reflects a profound emotional intelligence that is increasingly recognized as a cornerstone of personal and professional success.

The Importance of Emotional Intelligence

In the modern era, success is often measured by IQ, the traditional metric for assessing intelligence. However, growing research suggests that while IQ can predict academic achievements or technical skills, it is Emotional Intelligence (EQ) that plays a more crucial role in determining overall life success, career growth, and personal fulfillment. EQ refers to the ability to understand and manage one's own emotions and to navigate social relationships with empathy and grace. It involves skills such as self-awareness, self-regulation, motivation, empathy, and social interaction.

Emotional Intelligence doesn't diminish the value of IQ; rather, it complements it. Having a sharp mind is important, but it is the ability to connect with others, manage stress, and inspire people that often distinguishes the most effective leaders and successful individuals. In fact, according to research by psychologist Daniel Goleman, EQ can account for up to 90% of the difference between star performers and average performers in leadership positions. This means that while a "big brain" can help solve complex problems, it is a "big heart" that truly connects, inspires, and drives positive change.

A Tale of Two Employees: The Power of EQ in Action

To illustrate the significance of EQ in the workplace, consider the story of two employees: James and Lisa (names have been changed). James, with an IQ that would impress even the brightest minds, excelled in solving technical problems and tackling analytical tasks. Yet, he struggled when it came to teamwork and communication. His frustration often surfaced when colleagues didn't grasp his ideas right away, and his tendency to work in isolation left him disconnected from the rest of the team.

Lisa, on the other hand, had a more modest IQ but possessed an extraordinary level of emotional intelligence. She wasn't the most technically skilled person in the office, but she was attuned to her own emotions and the emotions of those around her. She listened intently to her colleagues, communicated with clarity and kindness, and handled conflicts with grace. Lisa's ability to navigate the emotional landscape of the workplace made her a natural leader, earning her the trust and admiration of her peers.

Despite James's intellectual brilliance, it was Lisa who advanced more rapidly in her career. Her capacity to connect with others, resolve conflicts, and inspire teamwork proved to be more valuable to the organization. This is not to say that James's intelligence didn't matter—it did. But Lisa's emotional intelligence allowed her to leverage the skills of the entire team, creating a more cohesive and productive work environment. In this way, EQ emerged as a key differentiator that propelled Lisa's success.

The Research Behind Emotional Intelligence

The importance of emotional intelligence is supported by a growing body of research. A study conducted by TalentSmart found that EQ is the single biggest predictor of performance in the workplace, accounting for 58% of success across various job types. The same study revealed that 90% of top performers have high emotional intelligence, while only 20% of low performers possess these qualities. The conclusion is clear: EQ is a critical factor in determining one's effectiveness, not just in leadership roles but in any position that requires collaboration and communication.

Moreover, higher levels of EQ are associated with better financial outcomes. Research published in the Journal of Organizational Behavior indicated that employees with higher emotional intelligence earned, on average, $29,000 more per year than their peers with lower EQ. This wage disparity reflects the value that organizations place on the ability to build strong relationships, manage stress, and resolve conflicts. Employees who can navigate the emotional dynamics of the workplace tend to perform better, receive more recognition, and are more likely to advance in their careers.

Real-World Examples of High EQ

Here are five examples of individuals who have demonstrated exceptional emotional intelligence in their personal and professional lives:

- **Nelson Mandela.** Nelson Mandela, the former President of South Africa and anti-apartheid revolutionary, is a prime example of someone who utilized high emotional intelligence to bring about monumental change. Throughout his life, Mandela faced enormous challenges, including 27 years of imprisonment for his efforts to fight racial segregation. Yet, he emerged from his time in prison without bitterness, instead advocating for reconciliation and unity. His emotional intelligence played a crucial role in South Africa's peaceful transition from apartheid to democracy.

    - **Empathy and Forgiveness**. Mandela's capacity for empathy allowed him to understand the fears and motivations of the very people who oppressed him. He famously invited his former prison guards to his inauguration as a sign of reconciliation, demonstrating his commitment to unity and forgiveness rather than revenge. This empathetic approach helped heal a divided nation and laid the foundation for a more inclusive society.

- **Emotional Self-Regulation**. Mandela's ability to control his emotions in the face of adversity allowed him to make rational and strategic decisions. His leadership was not driven by anger or resentment, but by a deep desire for justice and equality, which helped him win the respect and support of both his allies and former adversaries.

- **Richard Branson.** Richard Branson, the founder of the Virgin Group, is another example of a leader with high emotional intelligence. Branson's unconventional leadership style emphasizes fun, empowerment, and a deep respect for his employees. His EQ has not only helped him build a successful business empire but also fostered a culture of innovation and employee engagement within his companies.

  - **Empathy in Leadership**. Branson has always prioritized listening to his employees and understanding their perspectives. He believes that happy employees lead to happy customers, and this principle has guided his approach to business. Branson's empathy has made him an accessible and relatable leader, which in turn inspires loyalty and motivation among his teams.

  - **Emotional Awareness**. Branson's self-awareness and ability to understand his own emotional strengths and weaknesses have allowed him to make bold decisions with confidence. He is not afraid to take risks, but he does so with a keen understanding of the emotions involved, both for himself and those affected by his decisions.

- **Malala Yousafzai.** Malala Yousafzai, the youngest-ever Nobel Prize laureate, exemplifies emotional intelligence through her activism for girls' education. After surviving a targeted attack by the Taliban for advocating for her right to education, Malala continued her fight with even greater determination. Her resilience, empathy, and ability to inspire others have made her a global symbol of courage and hope.

  - **Empathy and Advocacy**. Despite the trauma she experienced, Malala's activism is not driven by anger but by a deep sense of empathy for other girls who face similar challenges. She uses her platform to amplify the voices of marginalized and oppressed individuals, always emphasizing the importance of education and equal rights. Her ability to connect emotionally with people worldwide has made her a powerful advocate for change.

- **Emotional Resilience**. Malala's ability to bounce back from adversity and use her experiences as a source of strength is a testament to her high EQ. She continues to channel her emotions into positive action, demonstrating how resilience and emotional intelligence can work together to create lasting social change.

- **Howard Schultz.** Howard Schultz, the former CEO of Starbucks, is known for his leadership style that focuses on emotional intelligence and creating a people-centric culture. Under his leadership, Starbucks grew from a small coffeehouse chain to a global phenomenon. Schultz's high EQ played a significant role in shaping the company's inclusive culture and social responsibility initiatives.

  - **Empathy in Business Practices**. Schultz has always emphasized treating employees (whom he calls "partners") with dignity and respect. He was one of the first CEOs to offer comprehensive healthcare benefits to part-time employees and invest in education programs for his staff. This empathetic approach has not only contributed to high employee morale but also to the company's overall success.

  - **Emotional Connection with Customers**. Schultz's vision for Starbucks was to create a "third place" between work and home where people could feel a sense of belonging. By focusing on the emotional experience of the customer rather than just the quality of the coffee, he was able to build a brand that resonates with millions of people around the world.

- **Jacinda Ardern.** Jacinda Ardern, the former Prime Minister of New Zealand, is often cited for her empathetic and emotionally intelligent leadership style. She has earned international praise for her compassionate responses to national tragedies and her inclusive approach to governance. Her high EQ has been evident in her handling of crises, such as the Christchurch mosque shootings and the COVID-19 pandemic.

  - **Empathy in Times of Crisis**. Following the Christchurch attacks in 2019, Ardern displayed immense empathy by personally consoling the victims' families and the Muslim community. She wore a hijab as a sign of respect and unity, and her empathetic words and actions helped heal a grieving nation. Her ability to connect with people on an emotional level has been a hallmark of her leadership.

- ○ **Effective Communication**. During the COVID-19 pandemic, Ardern's transparent and empathetic communication style helped New Zealand navigate the crisis more effectively than many other countries. She frequently addressed the nation with messages that combined facts with compassion, helping to reduce anxiety and foster a sense of collective responsibility.

What These Leaders Have in Common

While these individuals come from different backgrounds and industries, they share common traits that are indicative of high emotional intelligence:

- **Empathy**. They all demonstrate a deep understanding of the emotions of others, which allows them to connect with people in meaningful ways. They use this connection to inspire, influence, and lead effectively.

- **Self-Awareness**. High EQ leaders are attuned to their own emotions, strengths, and weaknesses. They leverage this self-awareness to make better decisions and maintain emotional stability during challenging times.

- **Emotional Resilience**. They all possess the ability to recover from setbacks and use adversity as an opportunity for growth. Their resilience not only helps them bounce back but also inspires others to do the same.

- **Effective Communication**. Leaders with high EQ know how to communicate in a way that resonates with others. They use language that is clear, empathetic, and motivational, which helps to build trust and foster strong relationships.

Practical Takeaways for Developing High EQ

The examples of Nelson Mandela, Richard Branson, Malala Yousafzai, Howard Schultz, and Jacinda Ardern demonstrate that high emotional intelligence is not limited to any one field—it's a valuable asset in business, politics, social activism, and beyond. Here are some practical steps you can take to develop your own EQ:

- **Practice Active Listening**. Make an effort to listen more than you speak. Pay attention to not just what people are saying, but how they are saying it. Notice their tone, body language, and emotions.

- **Cultivate Empathy**. Try to see situations from others' perspectives. Ask yourself how you would feel if you were in their position, and how that would affect your actions and decisions.

- **Reflect on Your Emotions**. Take time to understand your own emotional responses. When you feel strong emotions, ask yourself why and how you can respond constructively.

- **Learn to Manage Stress**. Developing techniques such as mindfulness, meditation, or exercise can help you manage your emotions better, especially in high-pressure situations.

- **Seek Feedback**. Don't be afraid to ask for feedback about how others perceive your emotional responses and leadership style. Use this feedback as a tool for growth.

Emotional intelligence is a skill that can be developed and refined, and by doing so, you can improve not only your relationships but also your overall effectiveness as a leader and communicator.

Applying Pooh's Wisdom to Your Life

So, how can you cultivate emotional intelligence in your own life and career? Here are some practical steps to help you embrace Pooh's wisdom and develop your EQ:

- **Self-Awareness**. Like Pooh, who acknowledges his own limitations with humility, begin by understanding your emotions, strengths, and weaknesses. Take time to reflect on your feelings, and consider how they influence your behavior. Journaling can be a helpful tool for exploring your emotional landscape and gaining clarity.

- **Self-Regulation**. Pooh may enjoy the occasional pot of honey, but he also knows when to take a quiet moment to think things through. Practice managing your emotions, especially during stressful situations. Techniques like mindfulness, meditation, and deep breathing can help you stay calm and centered. When you feel overwhelmed, take a cue from Pooh and go for a walk to clear your mind.

- **Empathy**. Christopher Robin's recognition of Pooh's big heart highlights the importance of empathy. Practice active listening by paying attention to what others are saying without interrupting. Try to understand their perspective and show that you care about their feelings. Being empathetic doesn't mean agreeing with everyone, but it does mean validating their experiences.

- **Social Skills**. Effective communication goes beyond just talking—it involves connecting with others. Work on building meaningful relationships by engaging in genuine conversations and being open to feedback. Like Pooh, focus on being present and showing interest in the lives of those around you.

- **Motivation**. People with high EQ are often driven by internal values rather than external rewards. Find what you are passionate about and let it guide you. Set meaningful goals and pursue them with purpose. Like Pooh, who is always on a quest (usually for honey), stay motivated by keeping your "why" in mind.

Creating an Emotionally Intelligent Workplace

Imagine a workplace where everyone embraces their inner Pooh—where kindness, empathy, and emotional awareness are as important as technical skills or strategic planning. Such an environment would foster trust, reduce stress, and boost productivity. When team members feel understood and valued, they are more likely to collaborate effectively and approach challenges with a positive attitude.

Organizations that prioritize emotional intelligence in their culture often see higher levels of employee satisfaction and lower turnover rates. When leaders exhibit high EQ, they inspire others to follow suit, creating a ripple effect that enhances the overall well-being of the company. By cultivating a culture that values emotional intelligence, businesses can unlock the full potential of their teams and drive sustainable success.

Beyond the Workplace: EQ in Everyday Life

The benefits of a big heart extend beyond the office. Emotional intelligence plays a crucial role in personal relationships, parenting, and social interactions. Whether it's resolving a disagreement with a friend, comforting a loved one, or understanding your own emotional needs, EQ can help you navigate the complexities of life with greater ease.

In friendships, having a high EQ means being able to listen without judgment, offer support without trying to "fix" everything, and express emotions in a healthy way. In parenting, it involves recognizing your child's emotional signals and responding with patience and love. By embracing the wisdom of a big heart, we can enhance the quality of our relationships and lead more fulfilling lives.

The Power of a Big Heart

The adventures of Winnie the Pooh may seem lighthearted, but they carry deep lessons about the importance of kindness, empathy, and emotional intelligence. As Christopher Robin wisely pointed out, Pooh may not be a bear of great intellect, but he is certainly a bear of a very big heart. In today's world, where the ability to connect, empathize, and navigate emotions is increasingly valued, having a big heart can be a powerful asset.

The next time you find yourself doubting your intelligence or abilities, remember Pooh's wisdom: it's not always the size of your brain that matters, but the size of your heart. By developing your emotional intelligence, you can open doors to new opportunities, strengthen your relationships, and find greater joy and success in both your personal and professional life.

Let your emotional intelligence guide you through the "forest" of life, and you'll discover that, just like Pooh, you already have everything you need to thrive. So take a moment to appreciate your big heart, nurture your emotional skills, and watch as they transform your world for the better.

BALANCE YOUR FOUR KINDS OF WEALTH

"Some people care too much. I think it's called love."

Winnie the Pooh

In today's world, we often equate wealth solely with money and possessions. However, Pooh's gentle wisdom encourages us to expand our understanding and recognize that true abundance comes from a balanced approach to life. Beyond financial wealth, there are three other kinds of wealth that play an essential role in achieving a fulfilling life: social wealth, time wealth, and physical wealth. By learning to balance all four, we can create a richer, more meaningful existence that goes far beyond monetary gains.

Understanding these four dimensions of wealth—financial, social, time, and physical—offers a holistic perspective on success and well-being. Each type contributes to the quality of life in its own way, and together they form the foundation for a truly abundant and balanced life. Let's explore how embracing this more comprehensive view of wealth can help us make better choices, cultivate meaningful relationships, and prioritize what really matters.

The Four Kinds of Wealth

When people think of wealth, they often equate it solely with money or material possessions. However, true wealth encompasses much more than financial assets. Understanding the different kinds of wealth can help us navigate life's choices and lead to a more balanced and fulfilling existence. The four kinds of wealth—financial wealth, social wealth, time wealth, and physical wealth—offer a more holistic view of success, one that goes beyond just monetary gain.

- **Financial Wealth (Money).** Financial wealth is the accumulation of money, assets, and investments that provide material comfort and security. It is often considered the most obvious form of wealth because it allows us to meet our basic needs, purchase luxury items, and enjoy various life experiences. Financial wealth can bring a sense of security, especially in times of uncertainty, and can offer opportunities for growth, such as education, travel, or starting a business. However, while financial wealth is important, it is not the only—or even the most crucial—factor in determining happiness. Studies have shown that after a certain income level (often cited around $75,000 to $100,000 per year), additional financial wealth has a diminishing effect on happiness and life satisfaction. This suggests that beyond a point, money cannot buy the fulfillment that comes from other forms of wealth.

Focusing too much on financial wealth can lead to stress, burnout, and neglect of other important life aspects. It's crucial to remember that money is a tool, not an end in itself. Use money as a means to an end. Consider how financial wealth can be used to enhance other forms of wealth, such as taking time off for a health retreat, investing in relationships through social activities, or purchasing time-saving services that free you to pursue your passions.

- **Social Wealth (Status and Relationships).** Social wealth involves the connections, relationships, and reputation we cultivate throughout our lives. It encompasses the influence we have in our communities, the recognition we receive in our professional circles, and the quality of our relationships with friends, family, and colleagues. Social wealth provides a sense of belonging, validation, and achievement. It can be deeply fulfilling to know that you have a positive impact on others and are respected for your contributions. However, social wealth can be fleeting if it's built on superficial values like popularity or social media status. It can also become a source of stress if we base our self-worth on the approval of others. Authentic social wealth comes from meaningful relationships and contributing to the well-being of others, rather than from chasing status or recognition.

Cultivate Social Wealth

- **Investing in Quality Relationships**. Focus on building deep and meaningful connections rather than collecting a large number of acquaintances. The strength of your social network often lies in the depth of your relationships, not the number of people you know.

- **Practicing Generosity and Kindness**. Giving your time, attention, and resources to help others can strengthen social bonds and create a more supportive network. This generosity often leads to reciprocity, making your social wealth more enduring.

- **Balancing Social Influence and Authenticity**. While it's natural to want to be respected or admired, ensure that your social wealth is based on your true self and values, rather than on trying to fit into a mold that doesn't align with who you are.

- **Time Wealth (Freedom).** Time wealth is the freedom to choose how you spend your time. It's the ability to pursue activities that bring joy and fulfillment, to relax and recharge, and to be with the people you love. Unlike money, time is a finite resource—once it's gone, it cannot be regained. This makes time wealth particularly valuable and often underestimated. Many people sacrifice their time for financial wealth, only to find later in life that they have missed out on experiences and opportunities for personal growth. Time wealth also plays a critical role in achieving balance across all areas of life. Without sufficient time, it's challenging to maintain physical health, build meaningful relationships, or even enjoy the financial wealth we've accumulated. As such, prioritizing time wealth can lead to a more fulfilling and content life.

Maximize Time Wealth

- **Set Boundaries**. Learn to say no to commitments that don't align with your values or goals. Protect your time as you would any other valuable asset.

- **Automate and Delegate**. Free up your time by delegating tasks or using technology to automate repetitive activities. This will allow you to focus on what truly matters to you.

- **Prioritize Experiences Over Possessions**. Studies show that experiences contribute more to long-term happiness than material items. Use your time wealth to create memories and enjoy life's moments rather than accumulating more things.

- **Physical Wealth (Health).** Physical wealth refers to the state of your health and well-being. It encompasses not just the absence of illness but the presence of physical vitality, mental wellness, and emotional balance. Good health enables you to enjoy other forms of wealth and live a full life. Without physical wealth, financial and social wealth lose much of their value because you may lack the energy or ability to enjoy them. Physical wealth requires a commitment to maintaining a balanced lifestyle that includes proper nutrition, regular exercise, sufficient sleep, and mindfulness practices to manage stress. Investing in your health pays dividends not just in terms of longevity but also in the quality of life you experience every day.

Build Physical Wealth

- **Establishing a Routine**. Create a daily routine that includes physical activity, healthy eating, and relaxation techniques. Consistency is key in maintaining long-term health.

- **Monitoring Your Health**. Regular check-ups and listening to your body's signals can help you detect issues early and address them before they become serious.

- **Incorporating Mindfulness Practices**. Mental health is a crucial component of physical wealth. Activities like meditation, yoga, or even simple breathing exercises can enhance both mental and physical well-being.

Integrating the Four Kinds of Wealth for a Balanced Life

True wealth is not found in just one of these categories but in the integration and balance of all four. Each type of wealth supports and enhances the others, creating a more holistic and fulfilling life.

- **Financial Wealth Supports Time Wealth**. When managed wisely, financial wealth can buy you time. This might mean hiring help for household chores, working fewer hours, or taking a sabbatical. However, if pursued excessively, financial wealth can consume your time rather than enhance it.

- **Social Wealth Enhances Physical and Emotional Health**. Strong social connections can improve physical health by reducing stress and providing a support system during challenging times. The emotional fulfillment from positive relationships also contributes to mental well-being.

- **Time Wealth Allows for the Pursuit of Health and Relationships**. When you have control over your schedule, you can invest time in maintaining your physical health and nurturing your social connections. This creates a positive cycle where your time, health, and social bonds reinforce each other.

- **Physical Wealth Enables Enjoyment of Financial and Social Opportunities**. Good health allows you to enjoy the experiences and activities that financial wealth can provide, and it gives you the energy to engage fully in your relationships.

Practical Steps to Balance the Four Kinds of Wealth

- **Conduct a Personal Wealth Assessment**. Evaluate how you are currently investing in each type of wealth. Are you heavily focused on one area at the expense of others? Identify where you need to rebalance your efforts.

- **Set Goals in All Four Areas**. Just as you would set financial goals, establish objectives for social, time, and physical wealth. For example, aim to spend a certain number of hours each week with loved ones, schedule regular exercise, or plan a period of downtime.

- **Adopt a Holistic Approach to Wealth-Building**. Consider how decisions in one area impact the others. For instance, taking on extra work for financial gain may detract from time wealth and physical health, so weigh the trade-offs carefully.

- **Practice Mindful Spending**. Use financial resources to enhance the other forms of wealth. For example, invest in health-related services or experiences that bring you closer to loved ones rather than accumulating more possessions.

- **Reevaluate Regularly**. Life circumstances change, and so will your priorities. Periodically reassess your balance across the four kinds of wealth to ensure that you continue to live a fulfilled life.

Rethinking Success

Understanding the four kinds of wealth—financial, social, time, and physical—offers a more nuanced perspective on what it means to live a successful life. True fulfillment comes from balancing these different types of wealth in a way that aligns with your values and goals. By focusing on all four areas, you can achieve a richer, more meaningful life that goes beyond monetary gain.

In the end, wealth is not just about what you have, but about how you live. When you integrate financial stability, meaningful relationships, time freedom, and physical well-being, you create a life that is truly abundant.

THE DANGERS OF BEING TOO SMART

"Those who are clever, who have a brain, never understand anything."

Winnie the Pooh

Winnie the Pooh may be known as a bear of very little brain, but his simplicity carries a profound wisdom that often escapes even the most intelligent minds. Pooh's approach to life is straightforward and unburdened by overthinking. He trusts in the power of simple joys, like a pot of honey or a stroll with friends, to guide him toward happiness. In a world that frequently values complexity and intellectual prowess, Pooh offers an alternative perspective: simplicity, curiosity, and intuition can often reveal deeper truths than complicated theories.

Interestingly, this idea is echoed in the teachings of Albert Einstein, one of the greatest scientific minds of the modern era. Though Einstein is often remembered for his groundbreaking theories and scientific contributions, his philosophy on life and problem-solving was rooted in simplicity. For Einstein, the true mark of genius was not the ability to make things complicated, but rather the ability to distill them down to their essence. His belief that "simplicity is the ultimate sophistication" finds a surprising ally in Pooh's uncomplicated worldview. Together, these two figures—one real, one fictional—remind us that the path to wisdom and discovery often lies not in what we add to a situation, but in what we strip away.

The Hidden Power of Simplicity

It is easy to assume that intelligence is synonymous with complexity. The more layers we add to a problem, the smarter we must be, right? However, as Pooh and Einstein teach us, there is immense value in simplicity. When Pooh sets his sights on a pot of honey, he doesn't get bogged down in overanalyzing every possible obstacle or complication. He knows his goal, and he moves towards it in the most direct way he can think of. If a tree stands between him and the honey, he climbs it. If the bees are angry, he might sing to them or find another clever way to distract them. Pooh's genius lies not in his ability to solve complex problems, but in his ability to simplify them, focusing only on the essentials.

Einstein expressed a similar sentiment when he said, *"Any intelligent fool can make things bigger and more complex... It takes a touch of genius—and a lot of courage—to move in the opposite direction."* True brilliance, according to Einstein, involves resisting the urge to complicate and instead seeking to simplify. It requires stripping away the non-essential elements and getting to the heart of the matter. This mirrors Pooh's actions in the Hundred Acre Wood, where he often finds that the shortest path to honey is a straight line. Pooh's success doesn't come from solving elaborate puzzles but from avoiding them altogether.

The Dangers of Overthinking

Overthinking is a trap that even the most intelligent minds can fall into. When we overanalyze, we may get stuck in an endless loop of considerations, possibilities, and contingencies, making it difficult to take decisive action. Pooh, on the other hand, approaches life with an almost childlike simplicity. When faced with a challenge, he does not dwell on the what-ifs or the complications. He simply follows his instincts, guided by his curiosity and a desire for honey. This way of thinking helps him to remain unburdened by unnecessary concerns, allowing him to enjoy life's simple pleasures without the weight of constant analysis.

Einstein understood the perils of overthinking well. He famously said, *"No problem can be solved from the same level of consciousness that created it."* This statement implies that when we face a challenge, we need to step back, shift our perspective, and often simplify our approach to find the solution. Einstein's theory of relativity, one of the most profound scientific breakthroughs of the 20th century, was not born from complex mathematical equations alone. It emerged from a simple yet revolutionary thought experiment—a reflection on what it would be like to ride alongside a beam of light. By reducing the problem to its most fundamental question, Einstein was able to unlock new insights that had previously eluded even the brightest scientific minds.

In this sense, Pooh's natural ability to cut through complexity with simple, direct actions serves as a practical illustration of Einstein's philosophy. When Pooh is stuck, he doesn't engage in endless planning; he changes his approach, tries something different, or asks for help. His way of navigating the world reminds us that we don't always need to "solve" our problems through intricate analysis—sometimes, we simply need to change our mindset or take a different path.

The Role of Curiosity in Discovery

Both Pooh and Einstein share a common trait: an insatiable curiosity. For Einstein, curiosity was the driving force behind all of his discoveries. *"I have no special talent,"* he once said. *"I am only passionately curious."* His breakthrough ideas did not come from a relentless pursuit of complexity, but rather from a deep fascination with the world and a desire to understand it in the simplest terms possible. He would often approach problems from a childlike perspective, asking "why" with the wonder and openness of someone experiencing the world anew.

Pooh's curiosity leads him on countless adventures in the Hundred Acre Wood. He doesn't set out with a detailed plan or an agenda; he simply follows his nose—or his tummy—and lets his inquisitiveness guide him. This open-minded approach often leads to unexpected discoveries and solutions, not because he has a perfect plan, but because he remains flexible and receptive to whatever comes his way. Pooh teaches us that we don't need to have everything figured out before we start. Sometimes, it's enough to take the first step and see where our curiosity leads us.

In the pursuit of knowledge or personal growth, we often feel pressured to have a clear, structured plan. But Pooh and Einstein remind us that sometimes the best discoveries happen when we allow ourselves to explore freely, without being constrained by rigid expectations. Curiosity doesn't always follow a straight path; it meanders, much like Pooh wandering through the forest. But it is precisely in that meandering that we may stumble upon answers we weren't even looking for.

Wisdom in Knowing What to Avoid

"A clever person solves a problem. A wise person avoids it." This quote, often attributed to Einstein, captures a subtle but crucial difference in problem-solving approaches. While intelligence often involves tackling problems head-on, wisdom sometimes means recognizing which problems are best left alone. Pooh demonstrates this wisdom naturally. He doesn't create unnecessary complications for himself; he focuses on what matters most to him—his friends, his honey, and the simple joys of life. He knows which paths to follow and which to avoid, not out of avoidance but out of an understanding that some problems simply aren't worth the effort.

Einstein's approach to problem-solving aligns with this idea. He believed that it wasn't enough to simply be able to solve difficult problems; the true challenge was to understand which problems were worth solving in the first place. His scientific career was marked by a constant search for simplicity and elegance, even when dealing with the most complex concepts. For instance, when he worked on the theory of general relativity, his goal was to find a simple, universal law that could explain the behavior of gravity. This search for simplicity helped him avoid unnecessary complications and led to one of the most elegant theories in physics.

The Path to Simplicity

In both Pooh's and Einstein's worlds, the pursuit of simplicity is not about avoiding hard work; it's about finding the most efficient and effective way to achieve a goal. Pooh's uncomplicated nature allows him to move through life with a sense of ease, focusing on what truly brings him joy. When he wants honey, he doesn't waste time considering all the possible ways to get it; he simply takes the most direct route available. While he might face a few bees or get stuck along the way, his path remains clear and uncluttered.

Similarly, Einstein's scientific achievements were grounded in the belief that the simplest solution is often the most accurate. His theory of relativity did not succeed because it was more complex than others, but because it provided a simpler and more elegant explanation for the nature of space and time. This principle can be applied in our own lives, whether we are solving a work-related issue, dealing with a personal challenge, or pursuing a goal. By focusing on the essentials and eliminating the unnecessary, we can make progress more effectively.

Embracing a Simple Approach in Everyday Life

So, how can we apply the lessons of simplicity, curiosity, and wisdom from Winnie the Pooh and Albert Einstein to our own lives?

- **Avoid Overthinking.** Recognize when you are adding unnecessary layers to a problem. Take a step back and ask yourself, "What is the simplest solution?" Sometimes, the best approach is the most direct one.

- **Stay Curious.** Let your curiosity guide you, just as it does for Pooh and Einstein. Don't be afraid to explore new ideas or follow unexpected paths. Curiosity doesn't always lead to a clear destination, but it often brings valuable insights along the way.

- **Know Which Problems to Avoid.** Not every challenge is worth your time. Be wise enough to recognize which issues are genuinely important and which are merely distractions.

- **Simplify Whenever Possible.** Whether it's a project at work, a conversation with a friend, or your daily routine, look for ways to make things simpler. Focus on what truly matters and let go of the rest.

The Art of Seeing Clearly

The wisdom of Winnie the Pooh and Albert Einstein converges on a single point: true insight comes not from complicating things, but from stripping away the non-essential. In a world that often equates intelligence with complexity, Pooh and Einstein remind us that clarity and simplicity are the real markers of understanding. Whether you are searching for a pot of honey or solving a complex problem, the principles remain the same: trust in simplicity, follow your curiosity, and avoid the traps of overthinking.

Pooh's seemingly simple adventures in the Hundred Acre Wood reveal a profound truth echoed by one of the greatest minds of the modern era: sometimes, the clearest path is indeed the best one. By embracing this approach, we can navigate life's challenges with greater ease, finding joy in the simplicity that lies at the heart of all true wisdom.

Embracing Intuition for Clarity and Guidance

"Don't be afraid to ask for what you want. Even if it's something as simple as a little quiet before lunch."

Eeyore

Understanding the Nature of Intuition

Intuition isn't about making decisions based on whims or magical thinking. Instead, it's the mind's ability to make quick judgments based on subtle cues and past experiences. It's our unconscious mind connecting the dots, recognizing patterns that may not be immediately obvious to us. It's that quiet voice within that nudges us when something feels right or warns us when something feels off. When we honor this internal guidance, we allow ourselves to make decisions that resonate with our true desires and align with our authentic selves.

Creating Space for Your Intuition

In today's hectic world, we are constantly bombarded with noise and distractions that can drown out our inner voice. Embracing intuition starts with creating moments of stillness, where we can hear the quiet wisdom within us. Whether through meditation, journaling, or simply taking a walk in nature, setting aside regular time for quiet reflection can help us tune in to our intuition. It's about making space for our inner guidance to emerge, even amidst the chaos.

Our bodies also have a way of reflecting our intuitive feelings before our minds catch up. Have you ever felt a sense of unease in your stomach, a quickened heartbeat when faced with a choice, or a profound sense of calm during a particular decision? These physical signals can offer valuable insights into how we truly feel about a situation. Paying attention to these sensations helps us connect more deeply with our inner knowing.

Letting Intuition Lead in Small Decisions

Learning to trust your intuition begins with using it in small, everyday choices. Whether it's choosing what to wear, which route to take on your way to work, or what book to read next, practice listening to your instincts. The more you tune in, the stronger your connection with your intuition becomes, making it easier to rely on when faced with larger decisions. Over time, you'll find that your intuitive sense grows sharper, guiding you toward choices that align with your values and desires.

The Interplay of Intuition and Rationality: Finding Balance

Intuition and rationality are not opposing forces; rather, they can work together to create a balanced approach to decision-making. Eeyore's wisdom shows us that intuition sparks insight, while rational thinking helps us analyze and apply those insights in a practical way.

When we let our intuition guide our initial thoughts and use rationality to refine them, we are able to make decisions that consider both emotional and logical factors.

Take, for example, the story of Steve Jobs. The co-founder of Apple often credited his intuition for guiding many of his business decisions. When developing the first iPhone, industry experts doubted the feasibility of a phone without a physical keyboard. However, Jobs trusted his gut instinct about the future of touchscreen technology, even though it defied conventional thinking. His willingness to follow his intuition, supported by rigorous analysis, ultimately reshaped the smartphone industry.

Trusting Intuition During Major Life Transitions

Intuition becomes especially valuable when we are facing significant life changes, such as switching careers, moving to a new city, or ending a relationship. These decisions often involve multiple layers of considerations—both practical and emotional. Trusting your intuition can help you navigate these complex moments in a way that honors your deeper needs and values. When Serena Williams, the tennis champion, decided to take a break from her sport to focus on motherhood, she did so because of an intuitive understanding of what was most important to her at that time. By listening to her inner voice, she was able to find a balance that allowed her to continue her career on her own terms.

Similarly, the poet and activist Maya Angelou spoke frequently about the power of intuition, describing it as a deep knowing that guided her actions even when others doubted her choices. By trusting her inner guidance, Angelou was able to live a life of resilience and authenticity, making choices that aligned with her true self, even in the face of skepticism.

Embracing Intuition for Personal Growth

Intuition isn't only about making decisions; it's also about personal growth and self-awareness. When we trust our intuitive insights, we open ourselves up to possibilities that we may not have considered otherwise. Albert Einstein once said, *"The intuitive mind is a sacred gift, and the rational mind is a faithful servant."* He acknowledged that some of his greatest breakthroughs, like the theory of relativity, were sparked by intuitive insights. These "aha" moments often come when we allow our minds to wander, free from the constraints of structured thinking.

Intuition invites us to explore new paths, to take risks, and to embrace uncertainty with a sense of trust. When we lean into that feeling, we allow ourselves to grow in ways that go beyond what is logical or expected. It is a way of honoring the deepest parts of ourselves, the aspects that truly know what we need, even if we can't always articulate why.

Practical Ways to Cultivate Your Intuition

- **Create Time for Reflection.** Make space for quiet moments in your daily routine. This could be as simple as five minutes of meditation, a walk in the park, or writing down your thoughts in a journal.

- **Pay Attention to Your Body.** Notice how different decisions make you feel physically. Your body often knows the answer before your mind does.

- **Embrace the "Aha" Moments.** When an idea or solution comes to you suddenly, trust that it has value. It may be the insight you've been waiting for.

- **Combine Intuitive Insights with Research.** Use intuition as a starting point, then validate your ideas with logic and data to create well-rounded solutions.

- **Acknowledge Intuitive Successes.** When your intuition leads you to a positive outcome, take note of it. This will build your confidence in your intuitive abilities.

Letting Intuition Be a Lifelong Companion

Eeyore's simple advice to ask for what you need—even if it's just a little quiet before lunch—reminds us that intuition is not about predicting the future or being reckless. It's about honoring a deeper understanding that is rooted in our experiences, emotions, and inner wisdom. It's about recognizing that sometimes, the answers we seek are already within us, waiting to be acknowledged.

As we navigate the complexities of modern life, let's remember to listen to our intuition and let it guide us in both big and small decisions. Trusting our inner voice doesn't mean disregarding logic, but rather, using it as a complement to our deeper insights. In doing so, we can find greater clarity, make more authentic choices, and live lives that truly align with who we are. Embrace intuition as a lifelong companion, and let it lead you toward a path of fulfillment and self-discovery.

EMBRACING RESPONSIBILITY OVER BLAME

"Don't blame me if it rains."

Eeyore

Though often known for his gloomy outlook, Eeyore's wry remark, *"Don't blame me if it rains,"* carries a profound truth that goes beyond the simplicity of the statement. It highlights the futility of blame and invites us to adopt a more constructive approach to life's inevitable setbacks. In today's world, where finger-pointing and assigning fault are common, Eeyore's words encourage us to shift our focus from blame to responsibility. Instead of getting caught up in finding fault or lamenting circumstances beyond our control, we can choose to take proactive steps toward positive solutions.

By embracing responsibility over blame, we gain a sense of empowerment, allowing us to navigate challenges with resilience and grace. Just as Eeyore accepts life's unpredictability without assigning fault, we too can learn to face life's difficulties by focusing on what we can do to improve the situation. Through this mindset, we cultivate a stronger sense of accountability and open the door to growth, peace, and constructive action in our daily lives.

Insight No. 1 — The Futility of Blame and the Power of Solutions

- **Eeyore's Insight.** Eeyore's view on blame is practical—rather than wasting time pointing fingers, he focuses on how to improve the situation. When he says, *"Don't blame me if it rains,"* he reminds us that some things are beyond our control, and it's more useful to find shelter than to assign fault.

- **Application in Modern Life.** In our daily lives, whether at work or in personal relationships, the blame game often distracts us from finding solutions. Eeyore's attitude encourages us to take a more proactive approach, focusing on solving problems instead of pointing fingers. By shifting our mindset from blame to responsibility, we empower ourselves to seek positive outcomes instead of getting stuck in negativity. For example, in a team setting, if a project doesn't go as planned, rather than blaming someone, focus on understanding what went wrong and how to fix it moving forward. This approach creates a collaborative and positive environment.

- **Practical Steps.**

  ○ **Redirect Focus**. When something goes wrong, skip the blame game. Instead, ask, "What can we do to fix this?"

  ○ **Take Responsibility**. Focus on your role in finding solutions instead of getting caught up in assigning fault.

  ○ **Promote Positive Alternative**s. Encourage discussions that center on constructive outcomes rather than dwelling on past mistakes.

Insight No. 2 — The Importance of Personal Accountability

- **Eeyore's Insight.** Eeyore hints that blaming others is not only useless but also weakens our personal responsibility. By owning our actions and reactions, we can handle challenges better and help create a more positive atmosphere.

- **Application in Personal Growth.** Ramandeep Singh's quote, *"We are a blaming society, yet we are a society. So, to make it a better place, we must change ourselves first,"* connects well with Eeyore's message. It reminds us that real change starts with looking inward and being responsible for what we do. If you face a tough situation at work or in your personal life, instead of blaming outside factors, think about what you can control and how you can help find a solution.

- **Practical Steps.**

  - **Reflect on Your Actions**. Regularly think about how your actions affect the outcomes you experience.

  - **Embrace Accountability**. Take responsibility for your part in any situation and focus on what you can do to make it better.

  - **Lead by Example**. Show personal accountability in your interactions, encouraging others to do the same.

Insight No. 3 — Moving Beyond Blame to Foster Emotional Resilience

- **Eeyore's Insight.** The Dalai Lama's saying, *"When you think everything is someone else's fault, you will suffer a lot. When you realize that everything comes from yourself, you will learn both joy and peace,"* resonates with Eeyore's view of life. By letting go of blame, we open ourselves to emotional strength and personal growth.

- **Application in Emotional Well-Being.** Blaming others often makes us feel helpless and frustrated. However, when we take responsibility, we regain our ability to affect outcomes and find peace in knowing we are actively working to improve our situation. If you're facing a tough relationship, instead of blaming the other person for the problems, think about how you can change your approach or viewpoint to create a more positive atmosphere.

- **Practical Steps.**

- **Shift Your Perspective**. Instead of focusing on what others have done wrong, consider how you can positively affect the situation.

- **Cultivate Emotional Resilience**. Realize that taking responsibility for your feelings and reactions brings greater inner peace.

- **Practice Mindful Reflection**. Regularly think about how your thoughts and actions impact your overall well-being.

Insight No. 4 — The Wisdom of Rising Above the Blame Game

- **Eeyore's Insight**. Epictetus, the Stoic philosopher, said, *"Small-minded people blame others. Average people blame themselves. The wise see all blame as foolishness."* This aligns with Eeyore's view, encouraging us to rise above the blame game.

- **Application in Conflict Resolution.** When conflicts arise, it's easy to start blaming others or even ourselves. However, true wisdom is recognizing that blame doesn't help. Instead, we should focus on understanding the root causes of the problem and work together to find solutions. In a workplace conflict, rather than getting caught up in who is to blame, try to understand each person's viewpoint and look for a solution that addresses the real issues.

- **Practical Steps.**

  - **Focus on Understanding.** In conflicts, aim to discover the root causes instead of assigning blame.

  - **Encourage Collaboration**. Promote a team approach to solving problems, where the focus is on finding solutions rather than pointing fingers.

  - **Cultivate Wisdom**. Adopt the mindset that blame is unhelpful and concentrate on achieving positive outcomes.

Insight No. 5 — Praising Over Blaming in Leadership and Relationships

- **Eeyore's Insight.** Catherine the Great's management style of *"praising loudly and blaming softly"* reflects Eeyore's practical outlook. By focusing on encouragement and helpful feedback instead of criticism, leaders and individuals can inspire positive change and create supportive environments.

- **Application in Leadership and Relationships.** Whether you're leading a team or building personal relationships, using positive reinforcement instead of blame can lead to more harmonious and productive interactions. By highlighting strengths and giving constructive suggestions, you foster a culture of growth and collaboration. As a leader, when a team member makes a mistake, use it as a chance to teach and guide instead of criticize. This approach not only helps them improve but also strengthens the relationship and builds a positive team culture.

- **Practical Steps.**

    - **Focus on Positives**. Point out strengths and achievements before discussing areas for improvement.

    - **Offer Constructive Feedback**. When criticism is needed, frame it as a chance to learn rather than just pointing out faults.

    - **Build Supportive Environments**. Create spaces where praise is common and blame is rare, encouraging growth and teamwork.

Embracing Responsibility and Solutions in Life's Challenges

Eeyore's insights on blame remind us that focusing on responsibility and solutions, rather than finding fault, enhances our personal well-being and social harmony. By stepping away from the blame game and adopting a proactive, solution-oriented mindset, we improve our own lives and positively impact our surroundings. As we apply these ideas in our daily lives, let's remember Eeyore's dry humor and deep wisdom, guiding us toward a future where positivity and proactive problem-solving replace blame and negativity. By embracing responsibility, we can face life's challenges with grace, wisdom, and a greater sense of fulfillment.

THE POWER OF A HUG

"A hug is always the right size."

Winnie the Pooh

When we first encountered this quote from Winnie the Pooh, it seemed like a sweet, straightforward message about comforting someone with a hug. In typical Pooh fashion, it conveyed a sense of warmth and simplicity. However, as we delved deeper into the significance of this statement, we realized it held layers of meaning, challenging us to think about connection, boundaries, and the evolving role of physical affection in our society. What began as a simple sentiment from a beloved bear became a journey through the intricacies of human interaction, cultural norms, and the timeless need for connection.

The Origins of Pooh's Wisdom

To understand the depth of Pooh's message, it helps to reflect on the origins of Winnie the Pooh himself. Created by A.A. Milne, Pooh first appeared in the London *Evening News* on Christmas Eve in 1925, in a story called "The Wrong Sort of Bees." Nearly a century ago, the cultural context surrounding physical affection was quite different from today. At that time, simple gestures like hugs were more universally accepted as expressions of warmth and comfort, often without the layers of scrutiny and boundaries that we now associate with them. The innocence and simplicity of Pooh's world reflected a time when a hug was not just an act, but a natural extension of compassion.

Fast forward to the 21st century, and the landscape of physical affection has changed dramatically. With a heightened awareness of personal boundaries, cultural differences, and issues of consent, what once seemed like an innocent gesture can now carry unintended connotations. This shift in understanding raises important questions about how we interpret physical touch, particularly in public and professional settings. Pooh's assertion that *"a hug is always the right size"* challenges us to rethink how we show care and affection in a way that is appropriate for the times.

Understanding Modern Sensibilities

In today's world, physical interactions like hugging are governed by a new set of social rules and expectations. The concept of personal space varies widely across cultures, and what may be considered a friendly gesture in one society could be perceived as invasive or inappropriate in another. In workplaces, schools, and public settings, the issue of physical touch has become increasingly complex. The U.S. Equal Employment Opportunity Commission (EEOC) defines sexual harassment as any unwelcome verbal, physical, or visual conduct of a sexual nature that creates a hostile or offensive environment. While a hug is not inherently sexual, it can be unwelcome if it violates personal boundaries.

This modern awareness has led to a reevaluation of physical gestures in professional settings. Many organizations now advise against physical displays of affection, such as hugs, to avoid misunderstandings or discomfort. The focus has shifted toward respecting personal space and seeking explicit consent before engaging in any form of physical touch. In this context, Pooh's advice about hugs must be adapted for contemporary norms. Instead of a literal embrace, we can think about what a hug represents: warmth, connection, and support. By doing so, we can reinterpret the message to fit the modern world while retaining its original essence.

Embracing Metaphorical Hugs

Given the changing attitudes toward physical contact, the idea of a metaphorical hug becomes even more relevant. When Pooh says, *"A hug is always the right size,"* we can expand this notion to mean providing emotional support, care, and understanding without necessarily involving physical touch. A metaphorical hug is a gesture of empathy and kindness conveyed through our actions, words, and attitudes. It is about offering comfort and reassurance in a way that respects personal boundaries.

In many ways, Pooh himself exemplifies this concept of metaphorical hugging. Throughout his adventures in the Hundred Acre Wood, Pooh's interactions with his friends are filled with simple acts of kindness, whether it's offering Piglet reassurance, helping Eeyore find his tail, or sharing his beloved honey. These gestures may not involve physical touch, but they convey a profound sense of support and love. The essence of Pooh's "hug" lies in his ability to be there for his friends, to listen, to empathize, and to share moments of joy and sorrow alike.

The Attitude of Gratitude

One of the most meaningful ways to offer a metaphorical hug is by embracing an *"attitude of gratitude."* Winnie the Pooh's appreciation for life's small joys is a recurring theme throughout his stories. He finds contentment in a pot of honey, delight in the company of his friends, and happiness in the beauty of the forest. This gratitude extends to the way he treats those around him. By valuing the simple pleasures and expressing thanks for them, Pooh's attitude becomes a kind of hug for the soul—a way of acknowledging the goodness in others and in life itself.

"An attitude of gratitude brings great things." (Yogi Bhajan)

Gratitude has the power to transform our interactions. When we practice gratitude, we are more likely to notice the positive aspects of our lives and the people in them. This shift in perspective can make our relationships richer and more meaningful. By expressing appreciation regularly, we give a metaphorical hug to those around us, reinforcing bonds and cultivating a spirit of kindness and generosity.

The Soulful Hug

"Thankfulness is like a hug for the soul." (Unknown)

This anonymous quote captures the essence of what it means to offer a metaphorical hug. When we express gratitude or show kindness, we touch the hearts of others in a way that can be just as comforting and healing as a physical embrace. A soulful hug acknowledges the presence, efforts, and contributions of those around us. It says, *"I see you, and I appreciate you,"* creating an emotional connection that transcends physical boundaries.

In times of difficulty or uncertainty, a soulful hug can be a powerful source of comfort. Whether it's sending a supportive message, offering to help, or simply being a good listener, these acts of kindness provide reassurance and show that we care. Pooh's wisdom about hugs encourages us to find ways to convey warmth and compassion, even when physical hugs may not be possible or appropriate.

Practical Applications of Metaphorical Hugs

How can we apply Pooh's wisdom about the power of a hug in our daily lives while being mindful of modern boundaries? Here are some practical ways to give metaphorical hugs inspired by Pooh's timeless teachings:

- **Express Gratitude Regularly.** Make a habit of thanking the people in your life for the little things they do. A sincere *"thank you"* can go a long way in making someone feel valued and appreciated. Whether it's a handwritten note, a text message, or a spoken word, expressing gratitude is a simple yet profound way to offer a metaphorical hug.

- **Show Appreciation in Small Ways.** Just as Pooh finds joy in a pot of honey or a walk with a friend, we can show our appreciation through small gestures. A smile, a kind word, or a thoughtful act can convey care and support, creating a sense of connection that is felt, even if not physically expressed.

- **Be Present and Attentive.** Giving someone your full attention when they're speaking is one of the most meaningful ways to show that you care. Being truly present, without distractions, communicates that the person matters to you. In a world where people often feel unheard, simply listening can be a powerful metaphorical hug.

- **Celebrate Achievements and Milestones.** Recognizing and celebrating the accomplishments of others, no matter how small, fosters a sense of community and belonging. Acknowledging someone's efforts or achievements is a way to say,

"I see you, and I'm proud of you." It's a metaphorical pat on the back or hug that validates their hard work.

- **Offer Support and Encouragement.** During difficult times, being there for someone can mean more than any physical gesture. Offering words of encouragement, checking in regularly, or finding small ways to help can be just as comforting as a hug. It shows that you're there for them and that they don't have to face challenges alone.

Hugs in a Changing World: Adapting Pooh's Message

While the societal norms around physical touch have evolved, the spirit of Pooh's message remains relevant. In today's world, where physical interactions are more scrutinized, the essence of a hug—whether literal or metaphorical—still carries the same warmth, kindness, and compassion that can make a difference in someone's day. A hug, in its many forms, is about human connection. It's about reaching out to others with an open heart, whether through a physical embrace, a thoughtful gesture, or an expression of gratitude.

Pooh's wisdom teaches us that the value of a hug is not in its size or physical form, but in the intention behind it. It reminds us to prioritize human connection and to find ways to show love and support that are appropriate for the situation. Whether we offer a physical hug to a loved one or a metaphorical hug to a friend or colleague, the message is the same: "You are not alone, and I care about you."

The Timeless Comfort of a Hug

"A hug is always the right size" is more than just a cute saying from a beloved bear; it's a reminder of the timeless power of human connection. In a society that increasingly values personal boundaries and individual preferences, Pooh's wisdom invites us to think creatively about how we can show warmth and care in ways that respect those boundaries. By embracing the concept of metaphorical hugs, we can spread kindness, gratitude, and comfort in a way that transcends physical touch.

In the end, what matters is not whether we give a literal hug, but whether we offer the essence of a hug—a gesture of love, support, and understanding. Winnie the Pooh, with his simple yet profound wisdom, reminds us that the world could always use a little more warmth, a little more compassion, and a little more heart. Let's carry that spirit forward, one metaphorical hug at a time.

Forever In Our Hearts — Embracing the Memory of Loved Ones

"If there ever comes a day when we can't be together, keep me in your heart, I'll stay there forever."

Winnie the Pooh

There is a gentle wisdom in Pooh's words that speaks to the deepest parts of us, especially in times of loss. These words took on a new meaning for one of the authors - Michael - after the passing of his beloved Aunt Mimi. Her vibrant spirit, her strong opinions, and her unwavering zest for life left a lasting mark on his family. Though she is no longer here in the way she once was, her memory remains a cherished part of his daily life, a quiet presence that brings both comfort and longing.

The Power of Memory and Presence

When someone we love is no longer with us, it can feel as though the world has lost some of its color. Yet, Pooh reminds us that those we love are never truly gone if we carry them in our hearts. Aunt Mimi's presence still feels close, woven into the fabric of Michael's life through the memories they created together. Each recollection, no matter how small, serves as a living thread that keeps her spirit alive.

In her later years, Aunt Mimi moved into an assisted living facility. Even there, her fiery determination never wavered. She joined a committee focused on improving the meals, voicing her opinions with the same lively spirit that had always defined her. It was a simple act, but it spoke volumes about who she was—a woman who, even in the smallest of circumstances, made a difference. When Michael thinks of those moments, he doesn't just remember her; he feels her with him. It's in these everyday memories, these small but significant moments, that we find our loved ones still beside us.

The Comfort of Cherished Memories

There's a quiet comfort in the small, everyday memories that rise to the surface when we least expect them. Michael often thinks back to their Saturday morning phone calls, where Aunt Mimi's voice would brighten his day with her infectious humor and love for Notre Dame football, the Yankees, and golf. Those conversations were not just routines—they were moments of connection, where laughter was shared, advice was given, and love was felt in the warmth of her words.

Helen Keller once said, *"What we have once enjoyed, we can never lose. All that we love deeply becomes a part of us."* Aunt Mimi is still very much a part of Michael, her influence showing up in ways he couldn't have imagined. Whether it's the sound of a football game on the TV or the taste of her favorite meal, these little things bring her back to him, if only for a moment. In the midst of loss, remembering the laughter and love they shared helps him find a sense of continuity, as though she is still here, sharing in life's simple joys.

The Timelessness of Love and Connection

Pooh's gentle reminder that memories are "living treasures" resonates deeply. They are not merely echoes of the past; they are part of our present, influencing our decisions, shaping our feelings, and guiding us through the days ahead. The love Michael shared with Aunt Mimi didn't end when she passed—it lives on in the stories we tell, the traditions we keep, and the moments we continue to celebrate in her honor.

Michael finds peace in knowing that by keeping her passions alive—her love for sports, her strong sense of justice, her appreciation for a good laugh— he is carrying forward a piece of her spirit. When he chooses to embrace the things she loved, he feels her presence guiding him, reminding him that her influence extends far beyond her time on this earth. It's not just about remembering; it's about living in a way that honors the connections that continue to shape us.

Cherishing Simple Moments and Lasting Bonds

As Pooh shows us, it's often the simplest moments that leave the most profound marks on our hearts. The everyday, seemingly insignificant experiences—like a shared cup of tea, a quiet walk, or a light-hearted chat—are the ones that stay with us. These moments with Aunt Mimi were where life's richness was found. They remind Michael that while the pain of loss is real, the comfort of cherished memories is just as powerful.

In those moments when he feels her absence most acutely, he holds on to the joy she brought into his life. Her sense of humor, her laughter, the sparkle in her eye when she was about to share a clever remark—these are the memories that help him celebrate the bond they had, even as he navigates the sadness of her absence. To remember her is not just to think of the times they spent together; it is to feel the enduring connection that continues to bring light into his world.

Embracing the Wisdom of Winnie the Pooh in Times of Loss

Pooh's gentle wisdom offers a unique perspective on loss, love, and memory. He reminds us that the smallest moments can leave the biggest impressions, and that love is a force that goes far beyond physical presence. When Michael reflects on Aunt Mimi's life, he finds solace in Pooh's teachings. He is reminded that she is not gone; she is in the stories he tells, the habits he's adopted, and the values he holds dear. Through their memories, she continues to shape his life, a constant source of love, laughter, and guidance.

As we journey through the complexities of life and loss, let us carry the wisdom of Pooh in our hearts. Let's hold onto the memories that bring us joy, celebrate the enduring bonds that connect us, and find comfort in knowing that those we have loved are never truly gone. They live on in our hearts, in the stories we share, and in the simple, quiet moments when we feel their presence with us. By embracing these teachings, we not only honor the legacies of our loved ones but also keep them forever close, where they will always remain—forever in our hearts.

THE POWER OF LISTENING

"Don't underestimate the value of doing nothing, of just going along, listening to all the things you can't hear, and not bothering."

Winnie the Pooh

In the quiet of the Hundred Acre Wood, where life slows down and the rush of the world fades away, Pooh teaches us something we often forget: the importance of simply listening. When Pooh talks about the value of *"doing nothing,"* he's not just referring to the act of sitting idly under a tree; he's talking about being fully present, about really tuning in to the moments we so often miss. To *'listen to all the things you can't hear'* means going beyond the spoken words and embracing the subtler whispers of life—the unspoken emotions, the quiet signals, and the spaces between words where true understanding resides.

A Simple Act with Profound Impact

One day, Pooh and Piglet found themselves sitting quietly under an old oak tree. It was one of those peaceful days when the only sound was the rustling of the leaves and the occasional chirping of a distant bird. As they sat there, Piglet began to open up about his worries, his fears, and the small things that troubled his heart. Pooh didn't interrupt, he didn't rush to give advice or solutions; he simply sat there, nodding gently and murmuring "uh-huh" from time to time. In that moment, without saying much at all, Pooh gave Piglet the gift of being heard. When Piglet finished, he felt a lightness he hadn't known before. It wasn't that his problems had vanished, but he felt comforted, simply because someone had truly listened.

This small story reminds us that listening is a powerful act of love and kindness. It is not about fixing things or offering solutions, but about being fully present for someone. Sometimes, the greatest help we can offer is to let someone feel truly heard, to give them space to express themselves without fear of judgment.

The Art and Science of Active Listening

In our busy, fast-paced world, genuine listening is becoming a lost art. Many of us fall into the habit of "listening to respond" rather than "listening to understand." Studies reveal that most people only remember about 25% of what they hear in a conversation, which indicates just how much we miss when we're caught up in our own thoughts or thinking about what we're going to say next. Dr. Ralph Nichols, considered the father of listening research, emphasized that listening isn't a passive activity. It's an active, engaged process that involves not just hearing the words, but truly understanding the message and the emotions behind it.

Listening requires more than just our ears; it requires our hearts and minds. It involves picking up on body language, tone of voice, and the underlying emotions that color the conversation. When we practice active listening, we don't just strengthen our relationships—we foster a deeper sense of connection and trust, allowing others to feel valued and understood.

Techniques for Deep, Heartfelt Listening

Pooh's wisdom encourages us to be present and patient, to embrace moments of quiet and listen with our whole being. Here are some techniques to help you become a more attentive listener, drawing from both practical research and the simple truths found in Pooh's world.

- **Engage to Understand, Not Just to Hear.** When you are listening, make sure your focus is on understanding the other person's message, not on preparing your response. Maintain eye contact and show that you are present through small gestures like nodding or softly saying "I see" or "uh-huh." If you find your mind wandering, gently bring it back to the speaker. Pooh's gentle "uh-huhs" weren't empty; they were little reminders to Piglet that he had someone's full attention.

- **Connect Heart-to-Heart.** Listening is about more than words; it's about connecting on an emotional level. Pay attention to body language and tone to understand how the speaker is really feeling. If someone's voice trembles or they hesitate, it might signal fear, sadness, or uncertainty. Acknowledge these feelings with a simple, *"That sounds really difficult,"* or *"I can tell this means a lot to you."* Pooh didn't need to say much to Piglet, but his patient and open presence conveyed all the understanding that was needed.

- **Remove Distractions.** In today's world, distractions are everywhere. Phones buzz, screens flash, and our minds are often somewhere else entirely. The next time you are in a conversation, put your phone away, turn off notifications, and be intentional about creating a space free from distractions. This act alone shows the other person that you value their words and are making the effort to be fully present.

- **Embrace Silence – It's Not Your Enemy.** Many people feel uncomfortable with silence in a conversation and rush to fill it. However, silence can be a powerful tool that allows the speaker to reflect and find their own words. It also gives you time to process what you've just heard. Pooh's quiet moments with Piglet weren't awkward—they were spaces where Piglet found the courage to share more, knowing he wouldn't be interrupted. Allowing pauses can invite a deeper, more thoughtful exchange.

- **Lean on Curiosity to Go Deeper.** Sometimes, the most profound insights come from asking gentle, open-ended questions. Instead of asking, *"Did that make you* *sad?"* you might say, *"How did that make you feel?"* This leaves room for the other person to explore their emotions in their own words. Be genuinely curious about their story—approach every conversation as an opportunity to learn something new about the person you're speaking with.

- **Reflect Their Reality Back to Them.** To ensure you have understood correctly, it's helpful to summarize what the speaker has shared and reflect it back in your own words. *"It sounds like you're saying..."* or *"What I'm hearing is that you're feeling..."* helps clarify any misunderstandings and shows the other person that you are actively processing what they are saying. This step is crucial in deepening the connection and making the speaker feel heard.

Oprah Winfrey's Legacy of Listening. Few people embody the power of active listening as gracefully as Oprah Winfrey. Her ability to connect with others on a deep emotional level has been a cornerstone of her success. On her talk show, Oprah didn't just ask questions; she listened. She leaned in, maintained eye contact, and responded not just with words, but with empathy. Her nods, her genuine expressions, and her thoughtful pauses created a space where people felt safe to share their stories. Her listening was a form of healing, offering her guests the rare gift of being fully seen and understood. Oprah's interviews reveal that listening isn't passive—it's an active and compassionate engagement with another person's reality. Her approach is a testament to the transformative power of truly hearing someone, and it's something we can all strive to bring into our own conversations.

Mahatma Gandhi — The Power of Quiet Listening. Mahatma Gandhi, the leader of India's nonviolent independence movement, was known for his remarkable ability to listen deeply to others. Gandhi's approach to leadership was rooted in his capacity to hear the voices of the oppressed and understand their struggles on a profound level. He spent countless hours listening to people from all walks of life—farmers, laborers, students, and even his political adversaries. His quiet, attentive demeanor during conversations created a sense of trust and respect. Gandhi believed that listening was essential for nonviolent resistance, as it allowed him to understand the grievances of the people and articulate a vision that resonated with the masses. By truly listening, he was able to identify the root causes of social and political issues and advocate for meaningful change. His approach to listening was not just about hearing words; it was about engaging with the emotions and underlying sentiments of those he led. Gandhi's ability to listen and empathize with the struggles of others made him not just a leader, but a symbol of peace and justice, whose influence transcended cultural and geographical boundaries.

Nelson Mandela — Listening as a Path to Reconciliation. Nelson Mandela, the former President of South Africa and anti-apartheid revolutionary, is celebrated for his skillful listening, which he used as a tool for reconciliation and healing. Mandela's 27 years in prison gave him a unique perspective on human nature and the power of listening. He often spoke about the importance of understanding one's adversaries, a belief he carried into his efforts to dismantle apartheid. Mandela made it a point to listen even to those who had oppressed him, understanding that true change could only come through dialogue and mutual understanding. When he emerged from prison and began leading the transition to a democratic South Africa, Mandela practiced what he called "deep listening." He engaged with former enemies, listened to their fears, and acknowledged their concerns. By doing so, he was able to build bridges across a deeply divided nation and pave the way for a peaceful transition of power. Mandela's listening wasn't just about resolving political conflicts; it was about acknowledging people's humanity, recognizing their pain, and working together toward a shared future.

Fred Rogers — Listening to Children with Compassion and Understanding. Fred Rogers, the beloved host of *Mister Rogers' Neighborhood*, was renowned for his ability to listen to children and speak to them in a way that made them feel valued and understood. He often said, *"Listening is where love begins,"* and his show exemplified that philosophy. Rogers listened to children not only with his ears but with his heart, creating a space where they felt safe to express their emotions. His calm demeanor, gentle tone, and thoughtful responses showed that he truly cared about their thoughts and feelings, no matter how big or small. Rogers' gift for listening extended beyond his young audience to the parents, educators, and caregivers who watched the show. He addressed difficult topics, such as divorce, death, and fear, with a compassionate understanding that made the experiences of children feel acknowledged and respected. He understood that children's emotions were complex and real, and he took the time to listen deeply, helping them navigate life's challenges with a sense of security. His approach to listening was revolutionary in the realm of children's television, creating an environment where empathy, validation, and unconditional acceptance were at the forefront.

These examples show that listening is not a passive act; it is a dynamic and transformative practice that has the power to heal, reconcile, and inspire. Whether it's Oprah creating a safe space for her guests, Gandhi listening to the voices of the oppressed, Mandela using listening to bridge divides, or Fred Rogers understanding the fears and joys of children, the impact of truly hearing someone is profound. These leaders remind us that active listening is an essential skill that can help us connect with others on a deeper level and foster a more compassionate world.

Embracing the Gift of Listening in Our Daily Lives

When we listen deeply and sincerely, we build stronger, more authentic relationships. In personal life, taking the time to truly hear a loved one's worries can be more comforting than any advice. In the workplace, listening with the intention to understand rather than to respond leads to better collaboration, increased trust, and more creative problem-solving. As parents, listening without judgment helps children feel valued and respected, encouraging open communication.

Listening is not just about absorbing words; it's about connecting with the emotions behind those words. When we listen with our whole hearts, as Pooh did for Piglet, we create a space where people feel valued, understood, and safe.

Pooh's reminder not to underestimate the value of *"doing nothing"* and listening to *"all the things you can't hear"* is more relevant than ever in today's noisy world. When we quiet our own thoughts, set aside our distractions, and tune in fully to the people around us, we create opportunities for deeper connection, understanding, and love.

So, the next time you find yourself in a conversation, practice being present. Engage with empathy, embrace moments of silence, and listen not just with your ears, but with your heart. It is in these moments of "doing nothing"—of setting aside our own agendas and simply listening—that we find the greatest power of all: the power to touch someone else's life and, in doing so, to enrich our own.

By learning to listen deeply, we are not only honoring the people we care about but also embracing a profound wisdom that brings us closer to our true selves. In the gentle art of listening, we discover that there is indeed great value in "doing nothing." Sometimes, it is in the stillness and the silence that the most beautiful connections are made, and the most meaningful conversations unfold.

THE POWER OF ACKNOWLEDGMENT IN EVERYDAY LIFE

"Thanks for noticin' me."

Eeyore

Eeyore, with his familiar gloom and dry wit, might have said *"Thanks for noticin' me"* with a hint of sarcasm, but there is a deeper truth hidden within his words. It speaks to a fundamental human need—to be seen, valued, and appreciated. Whether we are in the quiet meadows of the Hundred Acre Wood or navigating the hectic world of modern life, the simple act of acknowledgment can profoundly affect the way we connect with others and the quality of our relationships.

The Human Need for Recognition

Eeyore's quiet remark shines a light on a universal truth: everyone, no matter how self-sufficient or withdrawn they may seem, yearns to be recognized. It's not just about seeking attention—it's about feeling that our presence, our efforts, and our contributions matter. Even the most stoic individuals carry within them a desire to be acknowledged, not for grand achievements, but sometimes just for showing up.

In our everyday interactions, recognizing someone's efforts, whether it's a colleague's hard work, a friend's kindness, or a family member's quiet support, can strengthen bonds and foster a sense of belonging. In a workplace, for instance, taking a moment to genuinely thank a coworker for their contribution can boost morale and foster a positive, collaborative environment. It doesn't have to be elaborate; a simple *"I noticed how much effort you put into that project, and I appreciate it"* can have a lasting impact.

The Impact of Small Acts of Recognition

Acknowledgment doesn't always require grand gestures. In fact, the small, everyday moments often carry the most weight. It's the spontaneous *"thank you"* for a favor done without asking, or the appreciation expressed for a friend's listening ear after a difficult day. These small acts send a message that says, *"I see you, and I value what you bring into my life."*

Imagine a manager who makes it a point to compliment each member of their team on their individual strengths during a meeting. Not only does this create a culture where recognition is a norm rather than an exception, but it also motivates the team to keep striving for excellence, knowing their efforts won't go unnoticed. It's the same feeling Eeyore gets—although he may not show it—when someone takes the time to acknowledge him, reminding him that even his quiet presence matters.

Creating a Culture of Recognition

The habit of acknowledgment should extend beyond occasional moments; it can become a way of life. By integrating recognition into our daily routines, we foster environments—whether at work, home, or within our social circles—that thrive on mutual appreciation. It's not just about boosting someone's spirits for the moment; it's about laying the groundwork for stronger, more resilient relationships.

In the workplace, consider the practice of "Management by Walking Around" (MBWA), where leaders engage informally with their teams, not just about tasks, but about life. When a manager takes a genuine interest in an employee's hobbies, family, or well-being, it signals to them that they are valued as a person, not just for their output. It's as though the manager is saying, *"Thanks for being you,"* in the same way Eeyore's friends might notice his presence, even when he's quietly resting in the corner.

The Motivational Power of Acknowledgment

When people feel recognized, they are often more motivated to perform well, not just because they want to earn more acknowledgement, but because they feel valued and connected. As Simon Sinek suggests, effective leadership is not about seeking recognition for oneself, but about creating an environment where others feel recognized. When a leader makes a point to celebrate the successes of the team—whether big or small—it fosters a sense of unity and collective pride.

Think about the impact of a teacher who not only praises the star students but also takes the time to encourage the quieter, struggling ones. Those few words of acknowledgment can inspire a student to keep trying, to push beyond their comfort zones, and to believe in their potential. In this way, acknowledgment becomes a tool for empowerment, inspiring others to rise to their best selves.

The Ripple Effect of Appreciation

Acknowledging others not only uplifts them but also enriches our own lives. When we take the time to appreciate the strengths, efforts, or kindness of those around us, we cultivate an atmosphere of empathy and positivity. As Voltaire said, *"Appreciation is a wonderful thing: It makes what is excellent in others belong to us as well."*

Consider how this ripple effect unfolds: when one person expresses appreciation, it often inspires others to do the same. If you make a habit of thanking your coworkers for their contributions, they might start acknowledging each other more frequently, creating a culture of support and gratitude. At home, expressing appreciation for small daily tasks can make loved ones feel valued, leading to stronger relationships and a deeper sense of connection.

Finding Personal Fulfillment Through Acknowledgment

There is a unique kind of joy that comes from making others feel seen and valued. In recognizing others, we not only lift their spirits but also enhance our own sense of fulfillment and happiness. The act of acknowledging someone else's contribution is a subtle reminder to ourselves to practice gratitude. It shifts our focus from what we lack to what we appreciate, which can have profound effects on our mental well-being.

Even in the midst of a challenging day, taking a moment to thank someone can lift your own mood as well as theirs. It's a true win-win situation—what psychologists call a "helper's high," where performing acts of kindness or recognition triggers the release of feel-good hormones in the brain, enhancing our overall sense of well-being.

Embracing Eeyore's Wisdom in Our Daily Lives

Eeyore's simple yet profound *"Thanks for noticin' me"* isn't just a passing comment; it's an invitation for all of us to be more mindful in the way we interact with others. Whether we find ourselves in the quiet company of friends, like Eeyore in the Hundred Acre Wood, or amidst the busy rush of our daily routines, the power of acknowledgment can transform the way we connect with the world around us.

Acknowledging someone doesn't require grand gestures—it can be a smile, a nod, or a few kind words spoken at the right moment. It's about paying attention, being present, and making a conscious effort to notice the efforts, strengths, and presence of those around us. In doing so, we not only make others feel valued, but we also enrich our own lives with deeper relationships and a greater sense of purpose.

Let's take a page from Eeyore's book and remember to notice each other more often. A little acknowledgment can go a long way in brightening someone's day and reminding them that they matter. As we walk through life, let's strive to create ripples of recognition and kindness, transforming ordinary moments into extraordinary connections. It's these small acts of acknowledgment that weave the fabric of our shared human experience, making the world feel a little warmer and more connected, one *"thanks for noticin' me"* at a time.

THE ENDURING VALUE OF GENUINE CONNECTIONS

"After all, one can't complain. I have my friends."

Eeyore

Amidst Eeyore's familiar gloom and dry humor lies a heartfelt acknowledgment of something profoundly meaningful: the value of genuine connections. His simple statement, *"After all, one can't complain. I have my friends,"* reflects a truth that endures across time and circumstances—the importance of companionship. In a world often focused on achievements, material success, or individual pursuits, Eeyore reminds us that the true wealth in life is found in the people who share our journey. His words invite us to cherish these bonds, recognizing that friends not only bring joy but also offer strength, support, and a sense of belonging. As we navigate life's ups and downs, it is the presence of friends that adds depth and color to our experiences, making even the most challenging days a little brighter.

Insight No. 1 — The Evolutionary and Psychological Importance of Friendship

- **Eeyore's Insight.** Eeyore gently reminds us that friendship goes beyond just hanging out; it is a key part of being human that has helped us survive and grow. From the earliest times, strong social ties were crucial for our safety and progress.

- **Application in Modern Life.** Friendships are not just comforting; they are vital for our mental and physical health. They bring many benefits, both psychological and physical. Research from respected organizations like the Mayo Clinic highlights how important friendships are for our mental well-being and overall health. Friends boost our happiness, reduce stress, raise our self-esteem, and provide essential support during tough times, whether we're facing illness, loss, or personal challenges. When we go through hard times, having a close friend can make a big difference. Their support helps us handle difficulties with more strength, reminding us that we are not alone on our journey.

- **Practical Steps.**

  - **Cultivating Strong Connections.** Spend time and effort on nurturing and keeping supportive friendships.

  - **Lean on Your Friends**. Don't be afraid to ask for help when things get tough; your friends can be a great source of strength and comfort.

  - **Be There for Others**. Just as you rely on your friends, be there for them when they need help too.

Insight No. 2 — The Timeless Wisdom of Friendship

- **Eeyore's Insight.** Eeyore's thoughts on friendship echo the timeless wisdom of philosophers throughout history. Aristotle described true friendship as *"one soul in two bodies,"* highlighting the deep emotional and spiritual connection that goes beyond surface-level interactions.

- **Application in Personal Growth.** True friendships are rare and valuable, leaving a lasting mark on our lives. Eleanor Roosevelt wisely pointed out that many people may come and go, but true friends leave unforgettable footprints on our hearts. Mark Twain echoed this idea, believing that good friends, good books, and a clear conscience make up the essence of a good life. Thinking about the impact of a close friend who has stood by you during important life events can fill you with gratitude and fulfillment. These friendships shape who we are and help us navigate life's highs and lows.

- **Practical Steps.**

  ○ **Value True Friendships.** Recognize the special value of deep, lasting friendships and appreciate them.

  ○ **Express Gratitude.** Regularly tell your friends how much they mean to you and how they've influenced your life.

  ○ **Celebrate Shared Moments.** Take time to honor the memories and milestones you've shared with your closest friends.

Insight No. 3 — The Evolving Nature of Friendship

- **Eeyore's Insight.** Carl Cricco's thought, *"You can usually count your best friends on one hand; they may change over time,"* reminds us that while we might have few true friends, their impact lasts throughout our lives. Like Eeyore, who finds comfort in the company of Pooh and his friends despite his constant gloom, we also find that real friendships go beyond daily challenges, enriching our lives with shared experiences and lasting memories.

- **Application in Navigating Life's Changes.** Friendships can change as life evolves, but the bonds with true friends stay strong. Even as we grow and our situations shift, our connection with close friends deepens, offering us steady support and joy. Reconnecting with an old friend after years apart can show you how strong your bond remains, no matter how much time or distance has passed.

- **Practical Steps.**

  ○ **Adapt to Change.** Accept that friendships may change over time, but their true value stays the same.

- **Reconnect with Old Friends.** Don't hesitate to reach out to friends from the past; reviving old friendships can bring new joy and insights.

- **Embrace New Friendships.** Be open to making new friends that fit your current stage of life.

Insight No. 4 — The Role of Friendship in Professional Life

- **Eeyore's Insight.** Friendships don't just fulfill us personally; they also have a big impact on our work lives. The Gallup Q12 Employee Engagement Survey, which sparked some debate with its focus on workplace friendships, highlights their important role in boosting productivity and job satisfaction.

- **Application in the Workplace.** Colleagues who build supportive relationships not only improve workplace morale but also spark creativity and teamwork. This connection between personal and professional relationships shows how our social ties help us grow both individually and as a group. Working with a friend can make tough tasks more enjoyable and lead to more creativity and new ideas. The support you get from a workplace friend can also help you handle professional challenges more easily.

- **Practical Steps.**

  - **Foster Workplace Friendships**. Encourage and nurture friendships at work to improve collaboration and morale.

  - **Support Professional Growth**. Help your friends at work develop their careers by offering support and encouragement as they chase their goals.

  - **Balance Work and Friendship**. Keep a healthy balance between your work responsibilities and your friendships to ensure respect and productivity.

Insight No. 5 — The Synergy of Collaboration and Friendship

- **Eeyore's Insight.** The bottom line is that, as shown by both research and personal experience, we are more efficient and productive when we are surrounded by friends. This truth is reflected in my own journey as I write this book with one of my closest friends. Their presence inspires and encourages me, helping me overcome my doubts and fears, and boosting our shared creativity and determination.

- **Application in Collaborative Projects.** Working with friends not only improves the quality of the work but also strengthens the bond between those involved. The energy created through shared passion and support leads to greater creativity, productivity, and satisfaction. Co-authoring a book or collaborating on a project with a close friend can turn a challenging task into a rewarding and fun experience. The teamwork not only deepens your friendship but also results in a product that showcases both of your strengths and ideas.

- **Practical Steps.**

    - **Collaborate with Friends**. Look for chances to collaborate with friends on projects that match your shared interests and goals.

    - **Support Each Other's Growth**. Encourage and motivate one another to overcome challenges and achieve new heights.

    - **Celebrate Collaborative Successes**. Take time to recognize and celebrate the achievements you reach together.

Cherishing and Nurturing the Gift of Friendship

Eeyore's quiet thoughts on friendship remind us to cherish and nurture these meaningful connections in our lives. Whether during joyful celebrations or tough times, friends are pillars of strength, showing us empathy, loyalty, and unwavering support. As we explore the lessons of the Hundred Acre Wood, let's listen to Eeyore's wisdom and recognize that friendships enrich our lives in countless ways, creating a tapestry of shared memories and heartfelt moments that define our humanity.

In the larger picture of life, friendships are the threads that bind us together, crossing time and distance. They keep us grounded and lift us higher. Each friend we meet leaves a mark on our hearts, shaping who we are and who we want to be. They stand by us through life's chapters, sharing our joy and comforting us in sorrow.

As Aristotle said, *"A friend is one soul in two bodies."* This deep connection, based on mutual respect and understanding, gives us a sense of belonging and acceptance that is irreplaceable. Through these friendships, we learn empathy, resilience, and the true meaning of unconditional love. Let's embrace Eeyore's wisdom and the thoughts of those who share his insights, and treasure the friendships that make our lives richer, more meaningful, and deeply fulfilling.

EMBRACING SUNSHINE

"It never hurts to keep looking for sunshine."

Eeyore

Though Eeyore is often seen as the embodiment of gloom, his quiet advice to "keep looking for sunshine" carries a profound message of hope. In a world that can sometimes feel clouded by challenges and negativity, Eeyore's simple reminder encourages us to actively seek out the bright spots, no matter how small they may be. His words reflect an understanding that, while life inevitably brings its share of difficulties, there is always something good to be found if we choose to look for it. Embracing this mindset can help us build resilience, foster a positive outlook, and find strength amidst life's ups and downs. By focusing on the sunshine, we can navigate our days with a bit more optimism and grace, allowing light to guide us even through the darkest moments.

Insight No. 1 — The Practicality of Positivity

- **Eeyore's Insight.** For Eeyore, looking for sunshine isn't just about wishing for better days; it's a practical way of thinking that recognizes both light and shadow. He reminds us that shadows are simply areas without light, and understanding them is key to navigating life's challenges. Actively seeking out sunshine helps us find the strength and motivation to overcome obstacles.

- **Application in Modern Life.** Eeyore's idea is similar to finding the silver lining in every situation. Just as Coca-Cola started from a failed hangover remedy and 3M created Post-It Notes from a sticky mistake, Eeyore encourages us to see setbacks as chances to discover hidden opportunities. This mindset teaches us resilience and creativity, helping us keep going during tough times and think of new solutions where others see only failure. When you face a setback at work or in a personal project, try to see it not as a dead end, but as a new beginning. By changing your perspective, you might find new possibilities and solutions that were previously hidden.

- **Practical Steps.**

    - **Identify the Silver Lining**. In every challenge, look for potential opportunities or lessons that can help you grow.

    - **Embrace Setbacks as Learning Experiences**. See failures not as losses, but as valuable experiences that can lead to future success.

    - **Practice Creative Problem-Solving**. Use setbacks to inspire innovation, finding new ways to reach your goals.

Insight No. 2 — The Power of Optimism

- **Eeyore's Insight.** Walt Whitman's timeless advice to *"Keep your face always to the sunshine and shadows will fall behind you"* aligns perfectly with Eeyore's perspective. It highlights the power of optimism and positive thinking, suggesting that by focusing on the bright side, we can lessen the weight of life's darker moments.

- **Application in Daily Life.** Optimism doesn't mean ignoring problems; it's about staying hopeful even when things are tough. Helen Keller, who was blind, understood the importance of seeking sunshine. Her life, filled with remarkable achievements despite many challenges, shows how optimism and determination can overcome adversity. When you encounter a tough situation, instead of fixating on the negatives, think about the possible positive outcomes. This change in mindset can help you handle challenges more easily and with greater resilience.

- **Practical Steps.**

  - **Focus on Positive Outcomes**. When faced with challenges, look for the potential benefits or successes that could come from the situation.

  - **Cultivate a Positive Mindset**. Practice gratitude and positive thinking every day to strengthen your optimistic outlook.

  - **Surround Yourself with Positivity**. Engage with people, activities, and places that uplift and inspire you.

Insight No. 3 — The Role of Belief and Resilience

- **Eeyore's Insight.** Theodore Roosevelt's belief that *"Believe and you are halfway there"* supports Eeyore's message of hope and perseverance. It highlights the power of positive thinking in helping us reach our goals, even when we face challenges.

- **Application in Goal Setting.** Thomas Edison's thoughts on failure—*"Many of life's failures are people who did not realize how close they were to success when they gave up"* stress the importance of persistence and resilience. By believing in your abilities and staying committed, you can overcome obstacles that may seem impossible at first. If you're working toward a tough goal, remind yourself of your progress and how close you might be to success. This belief can boost your determination and keep you moving forward.

- **Practical Steps.**

- **Maintain Belief in Yourself**. Regularly remind yourself that you can achieve your goals, even when you face setbacks.

- **Stay the Course**. Commit to your goals, knowing that persistence is key to overcoming challenges.

- **Reflect on Progress**. Keep track of your achievements and use them as motivation to keep pursuing your objectives.

Insight No. 4 — The Impact of Perspective

- **Eeyore's Insight.** Wayne Dyer's idea, *"If you change the way you look at things, the things you look at change,"* fits well with Eeyore's philosophy. It encourages us to adopt a mindset of possibility and growth, turning setbacks into chances for learning and improvement.

- **Application in Shifting Perspectives.** Eleanor Roosevelt's wise words *"The future belongs to those who believe in the beauty of their dreams"* remind us that optimism and vision are key to progress and fulfillment. By focusing on our dreams and goals, we create a positive outlook that helps us move forward, even in tough times. When you're facing a situation that feels overwhelming, try to see it from a different angle. Think about what you can learn from the experience and how it might help you grow personally or professionally.

- **Practical Steps.**

  - **Reframe Challenges**. When you face difficulties, ask yourself how you can view them differently to find new opportunities.

  - **Adopt a Growth Mindset**. See challenges as chances to learn and grow, rather than as impossible obstacles.

  - **Visualize Positive Outcomes**. Regularly picture yourself successfully achieving your goals to strengthen your positive perspective.

Insight No. 5 — The Pursuit of Happiness

- **Eeyore's Insight**. The Dalai Lama captures the heart of Eeyore's philosophy with his belief that *"the purpose of our lives is to be happy."* In the face of life's challenges, Eeyore's advice to seek sunshine reminds us to prioritize happiness and well-being.

- **Application in Daily Fulfillment**. Happiness isn't just about success or material things; it's about our ability to stay positive and resilient during tough times. By focusing on the sunshine, we nurture a sense of inner peace and joy that goes beyond our circumstances. If you feel down or stressed, take a moment to think about what brings you joy whether it's spending time with loved ones, enjoying a hobby, or simply taking a quiet moment to reflect.

- **Practical Steps.**

  - **Prioritize Happiness**. Make choices that reflect your values and enhance your overall well-being and happiness.

  - **Focus on Joy**. Regularly do things that bring you happiness and fulfillment.

  - **Cultivate Resilience**. Build the mental and emotional strength to keep a positive outlook, even in tough times.

Embracing Sunshine as a Guiding Principle

Eeyore's unexpected wisdom teaches us to embrace sunshine not just as a metaphor, but as a guiding principle in life. Whether we are facing personal challenges, pursuing professional goals, or dealing with daily uncertainties, Eeyore's reminder to look for the positive helps us build resilience, optimism, and a mindset of possibility. By keeping our focus on the sunshine, we light our way forward, finding strength and inspiration to overcome obstacles and appreciate the beauty of life's journey.

In a world filled with shadows, Eeyore's wisdom shines as a reminder that there is always light to be found if we keep looking for it. By embracing positivity, we not only improve our own lives but also inspire those around us to seek their own sunshine, creating a ripple effect of hope, resilience, and joy.

THE DANGERS OF GROUPTHINK

"Before beginning a hunt, it is wise to ask someone what you are looking for before you begin looking for it."

Winnie the Pooh

This quote reminds us to seek clarity and personal understanding before rushing into group actions or decisions, helping to reduce the risks of groupthink. It highlights the importance of clear, independent thinking instead of blindly following the crowd or the group.

What is Groupthink?

Groupthink is a psychological phenomenon that happens within a group when the desire for harmony and conformity leads to poor decision-making. Members may ignore differing opinions, fail to critically evaluate options, or make irrational choices due to pressure to fit in. In organizations, groupthink can have harmful effects, stifling innovation, promoting unethical decisions, and leading to strategic mistakes.

Manifestations of Groupthink

- **Suppressing Dissent.** A key sign of groupthink is the suppression of differing opinions. In such an environment, employees often feel pressured to agree with the majority or a strong leader, leading them to hold back their own ideas. This echoes the saying, *"the squeaky wheel gets the oil."* With so many ways to share information today, it's easy for some messages to go viral. Often, these loud and extreme voices drown out more balanced perspectives. When we see the same message repeated on social media, it makes us think many must believe it's true. Some ideas we know to be only partly accurate, and it worries us that so many accept them. We urge everyone to take a few minutes to check three different sources to confirm what they read.

- **Illusion of Invulnerability.** Groups affected by groupthink often feel overly confident in their choices, ignoring risks and believing their decisions are flawless. This can lead to careless actions that overlook possible downsides. Just because someone is loud doesn't mean they're right. Use your experiences, skills, and gut feelings to question ideas, especially if they seem louder than necessary. The Bully Effect can occur more often than it should; confidence doesn't guarantee correctness.

Disregarding External Opinions. When groupthink is present, a divide often forms between those inside the group and those outside it. Opinions or feedback from outside are frequently met with doubt or hostility. This is where trust becomes important. Our internal networks have varying degrees of trust. If your friend and coworker Jack was wrong last time, you might question his information more in the future.

Consequences of Groupthink

- **Poor Decision Making.** Groupthink can lead to poorly thought-out decisions based on incomplete information. Without critical analysis, organizations might choose strategies that are flawed or risky.

- **Lost Opportunities for Innovation.** When employees feel they can't voice different opinions or suggest new solutions, creativity is stifled. Over time, this can seriously limit a company's ability to innovate and adjust to changing markets.

- **Ethical Compromises.** In a groupthink environment, members may downplay or ignore the ethical aspects of their decisions. This can result in choices that harm stakeholders, damage the company's reputation, and, in severe cases, lead to legal issues.

The Perils of Groupthink

- **The Space Shuttle Challenger Disaster.** One of the most tragic examples of groupthink happened during the 1986 Space Shuttle Challenger disaster. Despite serious concerns from engineers about the O-rings in cold weather, NASA managers were more focused on the political and public relations consequences of delaying another launch. The push for agreement overshadowed critical evaluations that could have prevented the tragedy.

- **The Bay of Pigs Invasion (1961).** The Bay of Pigs Invasion was a failed effort by the United States to overthrow the Cuban government led by Fidel Castro. Under President Kennedy, the U.S. supported a group of Cuban exiles in their attempt to invade Cuba. The operation relied on the belief that the Cuban people would support the invaders, which turned out to be wrong. Key advisors to President Kennedy were hesitant to express their doubts about the plan, leading to overly optimistic views of its chances for success. Concerns about the plan's feasibility and the risk of a major international incident were pushed aside. Instead, the group around Kennedy seemed to unite in support of the plan, failing to critically assess its potential risks. The invasion ended in complete failure, causing international embarrassment for the United States, strengthening Castro's position in Cuba, and further straining U.S.-Soviet relations during the Cold War.

- **The Subprime Mortgage Crisis (2008).** The 2008 financial crisis was partly caused by widespread investment in subprime mortgages and related securities. Despite clear signs that housing prices were unsustainable and many borrowers were risky, financial institutions continued to lend, package, and sell these unsafe securities. Many in the banking and finance industry, including top executives, seemed to ignore signs of an upcoming disaster, believing housing markets could do no wrong. Dissenting opinions were widely dismissed, and few challenged the belief that the rise in housing prices would last forever. The collapse of major financial institutions due to subprime mortgage exposure, along with government bailouts of banks, led to sharp drops in consumer wealth, major disruptions in financial markets, and a significant decline in economic activity, contributing to a recession.

- **The Ford Pinto Case (1970s).** The Ford Pinto, a subcompact made by Ford Motor Company, became infamous in the 1970s due to a design flaw that made its fuel tank likely to catch fire in rear-end collisions. Despite knowing about the problem, Ford initially chose not to change the design. Executives and engineers were aware of the Pinto's fuel tank issue before it hit the market but thought it was cheaper to settle potential lawsuits than to redesign the car. In meetings, those who had concerns may have held back their dissent because the prevailing view was that costs should be minimized, regardless of the risk to lives. This decision resulted in a series of tragic accidents and a costly legal battle for Ford. The Pinto case is often seen as a clear example of corporate ethical failure, causing significant financial loss for Ford and severely damaging the company's reputation.

- **Boeing and the 737 MAX Crisis (2010s).** The Boeing 737 MAX is a series of commercial jetliners designed and built by Boeing. In 2018 and 2019, two tragic crashes involving this model led to the worldwide grounding of the 737 MAX fleet. Investigations showed that a new software system called MCAS was a major factor in both crashes. Reports indicate there was significant internal pressure at Boeing to speed up the 737 MAX's development to compete with Airbus's new A320neo. This pressure created a culture where employees who raised concerns about the plane's design, including the MCAS, were often ignored or overruled. The focus on speed and cost savings seemed to overshadow thorough safety checks. The crashes resulted in the loss of 346 lives. Boeing's reputation suffered greatly, and the financial costs of grounding the fleet, compensating victims' families, and dealing with multiple lawsuits totaled billions of dollars. The crisis also led to a loss of trust among airlines and passengers worldwide.

- **Theranos.** Theranos, a health technology company led by Elizabeth Holmes, claimed to have transformed blood testing. However, it later became clear that the company's technology didn't work as promised, despite Holmes and other officials insisting otherwise. Inside Theranos, a culture reportedly developed where dissent was not accepted. Employees who questioned the validity of the technology were often ignored or intimidated. The board and investors seemed to trust Holmes without question for a long time, even as evidence showed something was wrong. The desire to believe in Theranos's groundbreaking promise, along with the fear of losing face or investments, led to an environment where tough questions were discouraged. The Theranos scandal resulted in a huge loss of investor funds, estimated at hundreds of millions of dollars. Patients received incorrect and potentially harmful health information, and employees lost their jobs when the company failed. Elizabeth Holmes was sentenced to prison.

Combating Groupthink: Strategies for Organizations

- **Cultivate a Culture of Open Dialogue.** Organizations should create an environment where employees at all levels feel safe and encouraged to share their opinions without fear of punishment.

- **Diverse Teams.** Diversity in demographics and thinking styles is a strong defense against groupthink. Different perspectives enhance the decision-making process.

- **Devil's Advocate.** Appointing a devil's advocate during team discussions ensures that the main opinion is thoroughly questioned, promoting a deeper analysis of decisions.

- **External Consultants.** Bringing in a third party to assess the situation can provide a fresh perspective and help spot any signs of groupthink.

Returning to the wisdom of Winnie the Pooh, *"Before beginning a hunt, it is wise to ask someone what you are looking for before you begin looking for it,"* we are reminded of the need for clarity and independent thinking. This simple yet profound advice highlights the importance of understanding and questioning before going along with group decisions, reducing the risks of groupthink.

Each case we've discussed shows how suppressing critical voices and blindly seeking consensus can lead to disastrous results. Strategies are needed to ensure decisions are well-rounded, critically examined, and ethically sound. By promoting an environment where dissent is not only accepted but valued, organizations can avoid the traps of groupthink and make better, more responsible decisions.

Our exploration of the dangers of groupthink emphasizes the need to balance individual thought with collective action. By following Pooh's advice, we see that asking questions and seeking clarity are vital steps in any decision-making process. Only by doing this can we protect against the dangers of groupthink and guide our organizations toward a future of good judgment, ethical integrity, and ongoing innovation.

THE ART OF CRITICAL THINKING

"Think it over, think it under."

Winnie the Pooh

Pooh's Lesson in Critical Thinking

In one of Pooh's many adventures, he finds himself in a tight spot literally. After eating too much honey, Pooh gets stuck in Rabbit's front door. At first, he tries to push and pull himself free, but it doesn't work. Only when he pauses to think and listens to his friends does a plan start to take shape. The answer is simple but effective: patience and time. Pooh learns that sometimes, the best way to solve a problem is to stop, think, and act calmly.

This story shows the importance of critical thinking—the ability to analyze a situation, consider different viewpoints, and make informed choices. Pooh's struggle reminds us that rushing to conclusions and acting without thinking can create more problems than solutions.

Understanding Critical Thinking

Critical thinking is the careful process of actively analyzing, evaluating, and combining information gathered from observation, experience, or communication. It involves questioning assumptions, spotting biases, and checking the truth of information before reaching a conclusion. This process is essential for making good decisions, solving difficult problems, and handling the challenges of daily life.

The Godfather of Critical Thinking: Charlie Munger

Charlie Munger, the vice chairman of Berkshire Hathaway and longtime business partner of Warren Buffett, is widely seen as a leader in critical thinking. Munger's approach to decision-making highlights the importance of thinking from different fields and using mental models.

Munger promotes a *"latticework of mental models"*—a framework that pulls from various areas like psychology, economics, history, and physics. By combining knowledge from different subjects, we can better understand complex problems and make smarter decisions. Munger's critical thinking skills have played a key role in his successful investment strategies and business ventures.

Additionally, The Critical Thought Lab (www.thecriticalthoughtlab.com) is an organization focused on promoting critical thinking skills. They provide resources, courses, and tools to help people improve their critical thinking abilities. The lab's mission is to encourage thoughtful analysis and informed decision-making, empowering individuals to tackle challenges effectively.

How We Think vs. What We Think

HOW we think is often more important than WHAT we think. The process of thinking critically involves questioning assumptions, considering different viewpoints, and using logical reasoning. It's about how we reach a conclusion rather than the conclusion itself.

Successful entrepreneurs like Elon Musk, Steve Jobs, and Jeff Bezos have all highlighted the importance of critical thinking in their decision-making processes.

- **Elon Musk. As** the CEO of SpaceX and Tesla, he is known for his first-principles thinking. This approach breaks down complex problems into their basic parts and builds solutions from there. Musk believes in questioning basic assumptions and using physics-based reasoning to innovate and solve problems. For instance, when he founded SpaceX, he challenged the idea that rockets had to be very expensive. By analyzing costs and components, he discovered that significant savings could come from vertical integration and reusability, changing the space industry.

- **Steve Jobs.** As the co-founder of Apple, he was a master at thinking differently. Jobs blended creativity with critical thinking, often drawing inspiration from unrelated fields like calligraphy and Zen Buddhism. His ability to connect different ideas led to groundbreaking innovations like the iPhone and iPad. Jobs stressed the importance of focus and simplicity, believing in removing unnecessary elements and honing in on core functionality and design. This approach required careful evaluation of every feature and decision, ensuring that the final product was both elegant and functional.

- **Jeff Bezos.** As the founder of Amazon, he uses a decision-making model called the "regret minimization framework." This method involves imagining oneself at age 80 and looking back on life. The aim is to make choices that reduce future regrets. This long-term view encourages thoughtful consideration and weighing potential outcomes before acting. Bezos also fosters a culture of high standards and critical thinking at Amazon. He encourages employees to challenge assumptions, debate ideas, and rigorously test their hypotheses. This culture has driven Amazon's ongoing innovation and growth.

Real-Life Applications

Critical thinking isn't just for high-profile entrepreneurs; it's a valuable skill for everyone. Here are some real-life applications and examples that show the power of critical thinking:

- **Healthcare.** In healthcare, critical thinking is crucial for accurate diagnosis and effective treatment. Doctors and nurses must analyze symptoms, consider patient history, and evaluate test results before making decisions. Critical thinking helps healthcare professionals avoid mistakes and provide high-quality care. A study published in the Journal of General Internal Medicine found that critical thinking skills are directly linked to better decision-making and patient outcomes. By encouraging critical thinking, healthcare providers can enhance their diagnostic accuracy and treatment effectiveness.

- **Education.** In education, critical thinking helps students analyze information, solve problems, and think independently. Teachers who promote critical thinking encourage students to ask questions, evaluate evidence, and consider different viewpoints. A report by the American Association of Colleges and Universities (AAC&U) highlights the importance of critical thinking in higher education. The report emphasizes that these skills are vital for students' success in the workforce and their ability to handle complex societal issues.

- **Business.** In the business world, critical thinking allows leaders to make strategic decisions, identify opportunities, and reduce risks. Companies that foster a culture of critical thinking are better able to innovate and adapt to changing market conditions. According to a survey by the National Association of Colleges and Employers (NACE), critical thinking is one of the top skills employers look for in new hires. Organizations that prioritize critical thinking benefit from employees who can analyze problems, create innovative solutions, and make informed choices.

We've all faced situations where we're stuck on a problem, and someone else comes along with a clear, logical solution. Often, they succeed not because they're smarter, but because they used a different way of looking at the problem. Here are some everyday scenarios where critical thinking can be applied:

Scenario No. 1 — Personal Development

Situation. Sarah, a mid-level manager, feels stuck in her career. She wants to move up but isn't sure how to develop the skills and mindset she needs.

Applying the Correct Mental Model. Sarah starts by adopting the "Growth Mindset" model, which emphasizes that abilities and intelligence can grow with effort and hard work.

Shift in Mindset/Paradigm. By embracing the growth mindset, Sarah changes her view from feeling stuck to seeing challenges as chances to grow. She begins to see her current skills as a starting point, not an ending point.

Action. Sarah enrolls in professional development courses, seeks feedback from her supervisors, and actively looks for new projects that stretch her abilities.

Change. Over time, Sarah gains new skills, builds confidence, and is promoted to a senior management position. Her proactive approach and new abilities also boost her job satisfaction and career path.

Scenario No. 2 — Emotional Intelligence

Situation. John struggles to manage his emotions at work, which leads to conflicts with colleagues and a tense atmosphere.

Applying the Correct Mental Model. John learns about the "Emotional Intelligence" model, which includes self-awareness, self-regulation, motivation, empathy, and social skills.

Shift in mindset/paradigm: John realizes the importance of understanding and managing his emotions. He begins to see his emotional responses as areas for improvement rather than fixed traits.

Action. He starts practicing mindfulness and reflection techniques to become more self-aware. John also attends workshops on emotional intelligence and begins to apply these principles in his daily interactions.

Change. As John develops his emotional intelligence, he notices a big improvement in his relationships at work. Conflicts decrease, collaboration increases, and John becomes known as a supportive and understanding colleague, enhancing overall team dynamics.

Scenario No. 3 — Leadership

Situation. Emily, a newly appointed team leader, finds it hard to inspire and motivate her team, leading to low morale and productivity.

Applying the Correct Mental Model. Emily adopts the "Servant Leadership" model, which focuses on the leader serving the team by emphasizing empathy, listening, and empowering others.

Shift in mindset/paradigm: Emily shifts from a top-down leadership style to one where she prioritizes her team's needs and development.

Action. She holds regular one-on-one meetings to understand her team members' goals and challenges. Emily provides necessary resources and support, encourages professional development, and recognizes her team members' achievements.

Change. Over time, Emily's team becomes more motivated and engaged. Productivity improves, and the team meets its goals more effectively. Emily's leadership style earns her respect and loyalty from her team, setting a positive example for others in the organization.

Applying Critical Thinking: Strategies and Tips

Developing critical thinking skills takes practice and intentional effort. Here are some strategies and tips to help you think critically:

- **Question Assumptions.** Challenge the norm and question underlying assumptions. Ask yourself why things are the way they are and whether there are other explanations. A mentor of mine always emphasized asking the one-word question, "WHY?" It's not about being troublesome, even though I have generated that reaction before. It's about digging into the root of the assumption. My least favorite answer is, *"Because that's how we've always done it."*

- **Seek Diverse Perspectives.** Consider multiple viewpoints and gather information from various sources. Engaging with different perspectives helps you see the bigger picture and avoid confirmation bias. After asking WHY, take it further and ask for other viewpoints, both high and low. Simon Sinek, a well-known speaker and author, uses this technique to simplify often complicated assumptions that are accepted simply because they've been repeated too many times.

- **Evaluate Evidence.** Assess the credibility and reliability of the information you come across. Look for evidence that supports or contradicts your beliefs, and consider the quality of the sources. I once found myself in a meeting with the IT and Web Development teams and asked if they could build a specific type of customer-facing website. Their first response was that it couldn't be done. I then showed them how a competitor was doing it, and they agreed it could be done, but it would take a lot of time and money. I asked, *"How much time and how much money? Then we can make a proper decision."*

- **Reflect and Analyze.** Take time to reflect on your thinking process and analyze your conclusions. Identify any biases and logical fallacies that may affect your judgment. There are entire books on this topic and even methods like Six Sigma. Six Sigma teaches the DMAIC process for evaluating feasibility and plausibility. DMAIC stands for Define, Measure, Analyze, Improve, and Control. It's a useful template that can be completed in just a few minutes.

- **Practice Problem-Solving.** Engage in activities that challenge your problem-solving skills. Puzzles, brainteasers, and strategic games can help sharpen your critical thinking abilities. Keep your mind sharp! Abraham Lincoln once said, *"If I had eight hours to chop down a tree, I'd spend the first six hours sharpening my axe."* This highlights the importance of preparation and the benefit of keeping our tools ready.

- **Seek Feedback.** Share your thoughts and ideas with others and ask for constructive feedback. Engaging in discussions and debates can help refine your thinking and provide new insights. The best ideas often come from unexpected suggestions. For example, I once asked a telemarketer how our latest mail piece was received by the target market. They said it was fine, but not something people tended to keep on their refrigerators. Our next mail piece was improved by adding a refrigerator magnet with a Call to Action, which helped us double our response rates with just a 10% increase in cost.

"Think it over, think it under." Pooh's simple advice carries deep wisdom for developing critical thinking. By taking a moment to reflect, question assumptions, and consider different viewpoints, we can make better decisions and handle life's challenges more effectively.

Embracing critical thinking allows us to uncover deeper truths, solve complex problems, and create meaningful change in the world. So, take a moment, think it over, think it under, and start a journey of thoughtful analysis and informed decision-making.

BEWARE OF SABOTEURS

"When you see someone putting on his Big Boots, you can be pretty sure that an Adventure is going to happen."

Winnie the Pooh

In the whimsical world of Winnie the Pooh, adventures are often sparked by curiosity and wonder, but they can also bring unexpected challenges. Sometimes, those challenges come not from Heffalumps or Woozles, but from subtle forces that seek to disrupt the harmony of the Hundred Acre Wood. These forces, known as saboteurs, can appear in different forms—people, circumstances, or even self-doubt—that intentionally or unintentionally undermine our efforts and bring chaos into our lives. Pooh's stories remind us that saboteurs may lurk even where we least expect them, making it all the more important to recognize their presence and strengthen our resolve. By embracing the wisdom found in the Wood, we can learn to identify these hidden threats, protect our peace, and foster resilience in the face of adversity.

Insight No. 1 — Recognizing Saboteurs in Disguise

- **Pooh's Insight.** Saboteurs come in many forms, sometimes appearing as friends or acquaintances who unknowingly or intentionally sow seeds of doubt and discord. These saboteurs may not always mean harm, but their actions can create obstacles and undermine our plans.

- **Application in Real Life.** Saboteurs can show up in unexpected places, often disguised as well-meaning friends or colleagues. For example, imagine a day trip to the cliffs of Dover where the weather forecast seems unfavorable. Doubts about the trip's success might arise not from nature's whims but from a friend who has different plans. Similarly, in a game of golf, a friend's withdrawal due to changing weather reports could unknowingly ruin the day's enjoyment. These examples teach two important lessons: always check your sources and understand the motives of those around you, and sometimes it's best to let things go when it comes to friends and family. When planning an important event or making a big decision, it's crucial to verify information and consider the motives of those offering advice. Recognize when someone's input might be influenced by their own interests rather than what's best for you.

- **Practical Steps.**

  - **Verify Information.** Always check the accuracy of information, especially if it comes from others who may have different motives.

  - **Assess Motives.** Think about why someone is offering advice or expressing concern: are they doing it out of genuine care or personal interest?

  - **Choose Your Battles.** With friends and family, sometimes it's best to overlook minor sabotage and focus on keeping positive relationships.

Insight No. 2 — The Deceptive Nature of Saboteurs in Business

- **Pooh's Insight.** Outside the Hundred Acre Wood, sabotage can take on darker forms. In business, some people try to harm others for personal gain, similar to a sneaky Heffalump spreading false stories to control the market.

- **Application in Professional Life.** Just like Eeyore's sad attitude can bring down his friends' moods, some companies or people spread lies to benefit themselves. A stock's price might rise after FDA approval, only to drop because of dishonest rumors aimed at causing panic for profit. This story highlights the harm caused by those with bad intentions. For example, in the stock market or any competitive field, be cautious of manipulation and lies. Do thorough research and depend on trustworthy sources before making decisions that might be influenced by false information.

- **Practical Steps.**

  - **Do Your Research.** Before making any big investment or decision, collect information from several reliable sources.

  - **Stay Informed.** Keep up with industry news and watch out for those who might spread lies for their own gain.

  - **Trust Your Judgment.** Learn to tell credible information from deceit, and don't let panic or rumors sway you.

Insight No. 3 — The Wisdom of Resilience and Unity

- **Pooh's Insight.** In stories of sabotage and deceit, there is a bright light of wisdom, like the sun shining through the trees of the Hundred Acre Wood. Just as Pooh and his friends stand together against challenges, we can protect ourselves from saboteurs by building a spirit of friendship and strength.

- **Application in Building Resilience.** After meeting an old man in Key West (not Ernest Hemingway), whose wisdom reminded me of Owl in his tree, I learned an important lesson: there are two kinds of people in the world. Some, like busy bees collecting honey, work hard to lift themselves and others. Others, like thistles in a field, try to bring down the joy and success of others. In both personal and work relationships, choose to be with those who encourage you, not those who try to undermine you. By creating strong, positive connections, you build a support network that can handle any saboteur's impact.

- **Practical Steps.**

    ◦ **Surround Yourself with Positivity.** Build relationships with people who support your growth and success.

    ◦ **Strengthen Your Network.** Create a strong, supportive community that offers resilience during tough times.

    ◦ **Resist Negative Influence.** Be cautious of those who bring negativity or try to sabotage your efforts, and distance yourself if needed.

Insight No. 4 — Protecting Peace and Harmony

- **Pooh's Insight.** The lessons from Winnie the Pooh remind us to be careful of saboteurs, whether they are old friends with their own plans or unseen forces in business. By keeping peace and harmony, like the unity among Pooh and his friends, we can face challenges and come out stronger.

- **Application in Daily Life.** In all aspects of life, from personal relationships to work, maintaining peace is essential. This often means being watchful for those who might disrupt that balance, intentionally or not. By creating an atmosphere of trust and support, we can protect ourselves from saboteurs and keep our connections strong. If you notice someone causing trouble in your social or work circles, address the issue directly. Encourage open communication and respect to stop further sabotage.

- **Practical Steps.**

    ◦ **Promote Open Communication.** Encourage honest dialogue to resolve conflicts before they get worse.

    ◦ **Foster Mutual Respect.** Create an environment where everyone feels valued, which helps prevent sabotage.

    ◦ **Stay Vigilant.** Be aware of possible saboteurs and take steps to protect the peace in your relationships.

The Strength of Camaraderie and Resilience

The Hundred Acre Wood, with its magical trees and lasting friendships, teaches us the value of unity and the need to be cautious of saboteurs. Whether they are old friends, tricky business players, or even our own doubts, these saboteurs can challenge our peace and success. However, by nurturing camaraderie, resilience, and awareness, we can shield ourselves from their influence and grow stronger, just like Pooh and his friends do.

As we face life's challenges, let's remember the wisdom of the Hundred Acre Wood: stay united, protect what is good, and look for the sunshine that can guide us through dark times. With these lessons, we can keep our friendships strong and our paths to success clear, no matter what saboteurs come our way.

THE GIFT OF TODAY

"Any day spent with you is my favorite day. So, today is my new favorite day."

Winnie the Pooh

On a bright, sunny morning, Winnie the Pooh decided to visit his dear friend Christopher Robin. As he wandered through the Hundred Acre Wood, Pooh hummed a cheerful tune, savoring the warmth of the sun on his fur and the soothing sound of the rustling leaves. When he arrived at Christopher Robin's house, he found not only his best friend but also Eeyore, Piglet, Tigger, and Rabbit, all gathered together for a picnic. They spread out a blanket on the soft grass and laid out pots of honey, sandwiches, and other tasty treats, settling down to share a meal and enjoy each other's company.

As they laughed, chatted, and shared stories under the canopy of the trees, Pooh felt a deep contentment wash over him. With a smile, he said, "Any day spent with you is my favorite day. So, today is my new favorite day." In that simple yet heartfelt declaration, Pooh captured the profound joy of being present, embracing the moment, and appreciating the company of loved ones. For him, happiness wasn't found in grand events or special occasions, but in the quiet magic of everyday moments spent together. The picnic turned into a cherished memory, not because of the food or the setting, but because of the shared experience of being fully present on that day together.

The Moral of the Story: Embracing the Present

Pooh's simple yet poignant words underscore the importance of living in the moment and valuing time with those who matter most. In our fast-paced, achievement-oriented world, it's all too easy to get swept up in the chaos of daily life—our thoughts racing ahead to future tasks or lingering on past mistakes. We often overlook the small joys that unfold in the present, missing opportunities to connect deeply with the people we care about. Pooh's wisdom reminds us that every moment is an opportunity to create memories, strengthen relationships, and find meaning in the here and now.

One figure who embodied this philosophy is Fred Rogers, the beloved host of *Mister Rogers' Neighborhood.* Fred Rogers was known for his authentic presence and his ability to make everyone he encountered feel valued and heard. He often spoke about the importance of appreciating each moment, once saying, *"The present moment is the only time we truly have."* This commitment to being fully present made him a cherished figure who taught generations of children and adults alike about the value of real human connection. Pooh's sentiment echoes this timeless lesson, inviting us to make each day our *"new favorite day"* by embracing it with our whole heart.

The Importance of Living in the Now

Living in the present, often referred to as mindfulness, is about focusing on the current moment with an open mind and without judgment. It means fully engaging with what is happening right here, right now, and appreciating the experiences as they unfold. Studies show that practicing mindfulness can significantly enhance our mental and emotional well-being. For instance, research published in the Journal of Personality and Social Psychology found that individuals who practice mindfulness tend to experience more positive emotions, higher life satisfaction, and better overall health.

Mindfulness also has the power to reduce stress and anxiety. In a study conducted by the University of Massachusetts Medical School's Center for Mindfulness, participants who completed an eight-week mindfulness program reported a 35% reduction in physical symptoms and a 40% reduction in psychological symptoms. This suggests that by simply focusing on the present, we can alleviate much of the stress that comes from worrying about the past or future.

The Benefits of Living in the "Now"

When we live in the present, we unlock several key benefits that enrich our lives:

- **Embracing Present-Moment Awareness.** Being fully engaged in the moment allows us to experience life more vividly. Instead of just going through the motions, we truly see, hear, and feel what is happening around us. This heightened awareness leads to a deeper appreciation of everyday experiences, turning ordinary moments into extraordinary ones.

- **Enhancing Mental Clarity.** Living in the present clears away mental clutter, leading to better decision-making and a clearer understanding of our surroundings. When we let go of regrets about the past or fears about the future, we free up mental space to focus on the present, enabling us to respond more thoughtfully and effectively to life's challenges.

- **Reducing Stress and Anxiety.** Much of our stress comes from ruminating about the past or worrying about the future. By grounding ourselves in the present, we can lessen these feelings of tension and worry, making it easier to navigate life's ups and downs.

- **Improving Relationships.** Being present enhances the quality of our interactions with others. When we give our full attention to loved ones, we foster stronger and more meaningful connections. People feel valued and understood when they sense that we are truly listening and engaging with them.

- **Boosting Creativity and Productivity.** Focusing on the present helps us tap into our creativity and productivity. When we are not distracted by thoughts of what has been or what might be, we can immerse ourselves more fully in the task at hand, leading to better results and a greater sense of fulfillment.

- **Achieving Greater Satisfaction.** Enjoying the present moment cultivates a sense of contentment. Instead of constantly seeking the next milestone or accomplishment, we learn to find joy in the journey itself.

- **Long-Term Benefits.** Mindfulness isn't just about improving immediate experiences. Over time, it supports a healthier, more balanced life by promoting long-term well-being, resilience, and emotional stability.

Being Present with Loved Ones

Spending genuine, quality time with loved ones is vital for building strong and lasting relationships. However, being physically present is not enough; we must also be mentally and emotionally present. This involves actively listening, which means fully concentrating on what the other person is saying, understanding their message, and responding thoughtfully. A study published in the International Journal of Listening found that active listening is associated with greater relationship satisfaction. Couples who practice active listening reported higher levels of intimacy and trust, underscoring the power of being truly present in our relationships.

Look at the story of Bill Gates's mother asking her son and his friend Warren Buffett about the secret to their success. They both answered in unison: FOCUS. This principle can be extended beyond business. When we focus on the present moment, whether in a meeting or with a loved one, we bring a sense of purpose and attentiveness that enriches the experience. Being fully present, even in the simplest of moments, can transform an ordinary interaction into something meaningful.

Overcoming the Challenges of the Digital Age

In our modern, technology-driven world, it's easy to be physically present while being mentally absent. Smartphones, social media, and constant notifications pull our attention away from those around us. A study by the Pew Research Center found that 89% of cell phone owners used their phones during their last social gathering, often reducing the quality of social interactions and leaving others feeling undervalued.

To counteract this, we must make a conscious effort to set boundaries with technology, especially when spending time with loved ones. By putting away distractions and focusing on the people in front of us, we show them that they are important and that we value the time we share together. When we give our undivided attention, we create moments that are not only more meaningful but also more memorable.

The Power of Connection and Authentic Presence

Dr. Brené Brown, a research professor at the University of Houston, has extensively studied the power of connection and vulnerability. In her book *Daring Greatly*, she emphasizes that being present is a fundamental aspect of building meaningful relationships. She writes, *"Connection is why we're here; it is what gives purpose and meaning to our lives."* Her research shows that individuals who cultivate meaningful connections and are fully present in their interactions experience greater life satisfaction and emotional well-being.

Additional insights from the Harvard Study of Adult Development, one of the longest studies on happiness, further emphasize the importance of relationships. This 80-year study found that the quality of our relationships is a key predictor of happiness and health. According to Dr. Robert Waldinger, the study's director, *"Good relationships keep us happier and healthier. Period."* These findings affirm that living in the moment and nurturing our connections are not only beneficial for our emotional well-being but also essential for a fulfilling life.

Applying the Lesson to Your Life

To fully embrace the present and strengthen your relationships, consider the following practical steps:

- **Practice Mindfulness.** Incorporate mindfulness techniques into your daily routine, such as deep breathing, meditation, or mindful walking. These practices help you stay focused on the moment and develop a habit of present-moment awareness.

- **Engage in Active Listening.** When spending time with loved ones, put away distractions and give your full attention to the conversation. Show genuine interest in what they are saying and respond thoughtfully.

- **Make Quality Time a Priority.** Plan activities that encourage meaningful interaction, such as shared meals, nature walks, or game nights. These moments allow for deeper connection and lasting memories.

- **Express Gratitude.** Regularly show appreciation for the time you share with others. A simple "thank you" or a heartfelt note can go a long way in strengthening your relationships.

- **Set Boundaries with Technology.** Designate specific times to be device-free, such as during meals or social gatherings. This practice helps ensure that you are fully present and engaged with those around you.

Embrace the Gift of Today

Winnie the Pooh's gentle wisdom encourages us to cherish the present moment and to find joy in the simple act of being with the people we love. By living in the now, we not only create meaningful memories but also deepen our relationships and enhance our overall well-being. In a world that often pulls our attention in countless directions, Pooh's reminder that "Any day spent with you is my favorite day" serves as a call to slow down, focus on what truly matters, and make every day our "new favorite day."

Embrace today with an open heart, be present with those around you, and make each moment count. By doing so, you will not only enrich your own life but also bring joy, connection, and meaning to the lives of those you love. In the end, the true gift of today is found in the moments we share and the memories we create together.

CHERISHING THE JOURNEY / BEWARE OF DESTINATION ADDICTION

"We didn't realize we were making memories; we just knew we were having fun."

Winnie the Pooh

Winnie the Pooh and his friends often find joy in simple activities.

One beautiful day, Pooh, Piglet, Tigger, and Eeyore decided to go on an adventure. They had no specific place to go; they just wanted to explore and enjoy each other's company.

As they wandered through the forest, they climbed trees, splashed in the stream, and had a lovely picnic. They didn't worry about where they were headed or what they would do next. They were fully present, savoring each moment and each other's company.

At the end of the day, as the sun set, Pooh looked at his friends and smiled. They had created wonderful memories without even trying, simply by enjoying the journey and each other's presence.

In our fast-paced world, it's easy to fall into the trap of "destination addiction" , the belief that happiness and fulfillment come from the next milestone, achievement, or phase of life. We often think, *"I'll be happy when I get that promotion,"* or *"I'll be content when I buy that house,"* or *"Life will be perfect when I find the right partner."* This mindset can rob us of the joy of the present moment, leaving us in a constant state of waiting and dissatisfaction.

Destination Addiction

It is often said that *"Success is a journey, not a destination."* Even in the Boston Marathon, crossing the iconic finish line is a success, but the real achievement comes from how you ran the race and, more importantly, how you prepared for it.

This idea subtly but powerfully changes our views on happiness and success. Many people believe that the grass is always greener on the other side, thinking true happiness lies in the next job, relationship, or grand adventure. While this mindset might seem harmless, it can lead to a life of constant searching, without ever finding peace or satisfaction.

As children, we're often taught to focus on the future. We hear questions like, *"What do you want to be when you grow up?"* or are told, *"Get good grades to get into a good college or find a good job."* This focus on the future can make us overlook the beauty and potential of the present.

Destination addiction leads to endless searching, where we never truly find the happiness we seek. Constantly seeking happiness outside ourselves can create a sense of ongoing dissatisfaction. When we're always looking ahead, we miss the beauty and potential of now. This cycle not only robs us of true contentment but can also cause burnout, strained relationships, and feelings of emptiness.

While pursuing future goals is important, it shouldn't overshadow the joy and fulfillment available in the present moment. Finding a balance between future aspirations and present happiness is key to a fulfilling life.

The Science of Destination Addiction

Here are some research findings that highlight the effects of destination addiction:

- **The Hedonic Treadmill Effect.** A Study by Brickman and Campbell (1971) introduced the idea of the "hedonic treadmill," which suggests that people tend to return to a baseline level of happiness, no matter what positive or negative changes occur in their lives. Constantly seeking new achievements or possessions for happiness is pointless, as our satisfaction from these gains is usually short-lived. This connects to destination addiction, where people believe future accomplishments will bring lasting happiness, only to find they return to their original level of contentment.

- **The Paradox of Choice.** Research by Barry Schwartz (2004), especially in his book "The Paradox of Choice," shows that having too many choices can lead to anxiety and dissatisfaction. People often think more options will make them happier, but it can actually cause decision paralysis and regret. Destination addiction can be fueled by the belief that the next choice or opportunity will bring ultimate happiness. However, Schwartz's findings suggest that this mindset can lead to constant second-guessing and disappointment.

- **Future Orientation and Well-being.** A Study by Boniwell, Osin, Linley, and Ivanchenko (2010) looked at the link between how we think about time and our well-being. It found that while focusing on the future can help with goal-setting and planning, excessive attention to the future can hurt our well-being. People with destination addiction often focus on future achievements rather than present experiences, which can lower their overall happiness and satisfaction.

- **Mindfulness and Present-Moment Awareness.** Research by Brown and Ryan (2003) on mindfulness showed that being aware of the present moment has positive effects on mental well-being. Mindfulness practices help people focus on the here and now, reducing anxiety and improving life satisfaction. Practicing mindfulness can counteract the negative effects of destination addiction by encouraging people to appreciate and enjoy their current circumstances.

- **Temporal Comparison Theory.** A study by Wilson and Ross (2001) suggests that people often compare their current selves to their past or future selves. While these comparisons can motivate self-improvement, they can also lead to dissatisfaction if people think their future selves will be much happier or more successful. Destination addiction is often fueled by negative comparisons between the present and an idealized future. This can create a cycle of dissatisfaction, where the present never feels good enough compared to a constantly changing future goal.

- **Impact of Goal Attainment on Happiness.** Research by Emmons and McCullough (2003) on personal goals and happiness found that while setting and achieving goals can boost happiness, the effect is usually short-lived. Constantly setting new goals without appreciating the present can lead to a never-ending cycle of seeking. This finding highlights the essence of destination addiction—believing that each new goal will bring lasting happiness, only to discover that the satisfaction is temporary.

Practical Tips for Overcoming Destination Addiction

- **Cultivate Gratitude for the Present.** Make it a daily habit to think about what you're thankful for. This practice can help you enjoy the moment and find happiness in the now; e.g., keep a gratitude journal where you write down things that make you happy each day. This simple habit can shift your focus from what you lack to what you already have.

- **Engage Fully in the Present.** Be mindful of what you're doing each day and enjoy it. Whether you're eating a meal, spending time with family, or working on a project, try to be fully present; e.g., when eating, pay attention to the flavors, textures, and smells. Avoid distractions like checking your phone or watching TV.

- **Set Realistic Goals.** It's good to have goals, but make sure they are realistic. Break them down into smaller steps so you can celebrate small successes along the way; e.g., if you want to run a marathon, start by aiming to run a 5K. Celebrate your progress and enjoy the training journey.

- **Create a "Right Here, Right Now" List.** This exercise helps you focus on the present and appreciate what you have achieved and what brings you joy now; e.g. write down things that make you happy, lessons you're learning, what you like about yourself, and the progress you're making toward your goals.

- **Practice Mindfulness.** Mindfulness exercises can help you stay in the present. Activities like meditation, deep breathing, and mindful walking can increase your awareness of now; e.g., spend a few minutes each day meditating. Focus on your breath and gently bring your mind back to the present whenever it starts to wander.

Destination addiction can lead us to endlessly search for happiness without ever truly finding it. By understanding its downsides, valuing our achievements, and appreciating our relationships, we can discover a deep and lasting contentment. Remember, true happiness isn't about where you're headed; it's about enjoying where you are.

As Winnie the Pooh wisely says, *"We didn't realize we were making memories, we just knew we were having fun."* By focusing on the journey instead of the destination, we can create wonderful memories and find joy in the present. So, the next time you catch yourself fixating on a future goal, take a moment to appreciate the here and now. Your future self will thank you for it.

CONCLUSION: LIFE LESSONS FROM WINNIE THE POOH

As we journeyed through the timeless stories of Winnie the Pooh, we've discovered a wealth of wisdom about personal growth, mindset, and living a fulfilling life.

While we didn't refer to all of the characters from the Hundred Acre Wood in this book, here's a brief look at how these beloved characters and their adventures in the Hundred Acre Wood can deeply influence our perspectives and actions in many areas of life.

Personal Growth and Self-Improvement

Winnie the Pooh and his friends show us personal growth in simple yet profound ways. Each character has unique traits that offer valuable lessons in self-improvement.

- **Winnie the Pooh**. Pooh's contentment with who he is teaches us about self-acceptance. Though he may not be the smartest, Pooh embraces his abilities and makes the most of his situation. His love for honey, while sometimes causing trouble, also reflects his commitment to what makes him happy. This reminds us to pursue our passions with enthusiasm and accept our limitations with grace.

- **Piglet**. Piglet's journey is about overcoming fear and growing in courage. Even though he's small and timid, Piglet often steps up when challenges arise, especially to help his friends. His bravery encourages us to step out of our comfort zones and embrace growth, no matter how scary it seems.

- **Eeyore**. Eeyore's constant sadness is a contrast to the others, yet he's still a valued member of the group. His story reminds us that personal growth sometimes involves accepting and managing our emotional struggles. It teaches us that it's okay to have bad days and that our worth isn't lessened by our sadness.

Mindset and Attitude

The residents of the Hundred Acre Wood each have a unique mindset and attitude, shaping how they interact with others and handle challenges. Their stories highlight the power of a positive mindset and the need to maintain a balanced attitude.

- **Tigger**. Tigger's endless energy and enthusiasm show the strength of a positive attitude. His constant bouncing and excitement remind us to approach life with joy and optimism. But Tigger also learns that it's important to consider others' feelings and realize that his energy isn't always appropriate. Finding this balance is key to having healthy relationships.

- **Rabbit**. Rabbit's careful and sometimes controlling nature teaches us the downside of being too rigid. While his organization skills are impressive, his need for control often leads to frustration. Rabbit's experiences remind us to be flexible and to adjust our mindset when life doesn't go as planned.

- **Christopher Robin**. As the leader and problem-solver, Christopher Robin represents wisdom and kindness. His caring attitude and ability to solve problems with compassion show us the importance of leading with empathy and staying positive, even when faced with tough situations.

Wisdom and Philosophy

The simple yet meaningful words and actions of Pooh and his friends often express deep philosophical insights.

- **Pooh's Zen**. Pooh's relaxed approach to life and his ability to enjoy the present moment reflect a Zen-like way of thinking. His famous line, "Sometimes the smallest things take up the most room in your heart," highlights the importance of appreciating life's simple pleasures. Pooh's wisdom is in his ability to live in the moment and find contentment with what he has.

- **Owl's Knowledge**. Owl, with his wealth of knowledge and love for storytelling, represents the pursuit of wisdom. But his occasional confusion and mistakes remind us that wisdom isn't just about knowing things; it's also about understanding and humility. Owl teaches us to seek knowledge while staying open to learning from our own mistakes.

Relationships and Communication

The interactions between Pooh and his friends show the importance of strong relationships and effective communication.

- **Pooh and Piglet**. The deep friendship between Pooh and Piglet shows loyalty and support. Their bond reminds us how important it is to be there for each other, to listen, and to offer comfort. This relationship highlights the value of empathy and understanding in building strong connections.

- **Kanga and Roo**. The mother-child relationship between Kanga and Roo demonstrates nurturing and guidance. Kanga's gentle care and Roo's adventurous spirit show the balance between offering support and allowing independence. This teaches us to nurture our relationships while also encouraging personal growth.

- **The Group's Adventures**. The adventures and misadventures of the Hundred Acre Wood group show the importance of teamwork and communication. Whether they're looking for Eeyore's lost tail or trying to trap a Heffalump, their success depends on working together and communicating well. These stories remind us that collaboration and open communication are key to reaching shared goals.

Critical Thinking and Decision Making

The decision-making processes of Pooh and his friends, while often playful, offer valuable lessons in critical thinking and problem-solving.

- **Pooh's Intuition**. Pooh often listens to his "tummy" to guide his choices, which represents intuitive thinking. While this may not always be the most logical approach, it teaches us to trust our instincts and understand that intuition can be a helpful guide in certain situations.

- **Rabbit's Planning**. Rabbit's careful approach to problem-solving contrasts with Pooh's intuition. His need to plan and organize highlights the importance of critical thinking and preparation. However, his experiences also show that overthinking can sometimes get in the way of taking action. Finding a balance between intuition and careful planning is essential for effective decision-making.

- **Group Problem-Solving**. Many adventures in the Hundred Acre Wood involve working together to solve problems, where each character's unique perspective helps find the solution. These stories emphasize the importance of different viewpoints and teamwork in making well-rounded decisions.

Simplicity and Minimalism

The simple lives of Pooh and his friends highlight the beauty of minimalism and the fulfillment it brings.

- **Pooh's Simple Pleasures**. Pooh's love for honey and simple joys reflects the idea of minimalism. His contentment with the basics teaches us that happiness doesn't come from owning many things but from appreciating what we have. Embracing simplicity can lead to a more fulfilling and less stressful life.

- **Eeyore's Minimalism**. Eeyore's modest lifestyle, despite his sadness, shows that one can find contentment with very little. His simple home and lack of material desires remind us that minimalism isn't about going without; it's about finding joy in simplicity.

Living in the Present

One of the most important lessons from the Hundred Acre Wood is the value of living in the present moment.

- **Pooh's Present Focus**. Pooh's ability to enjoy the present, whether he's eating honey or spending time with friends, shows the essence of mindfulness. His actions teach us to savor each moment and not to get caught up in worries about the past or future.

- **Piglet's Anxiety and Growth**. Piglet's journey from anxiety to courage highlights the importance of focusing on the present to overcome fears. By staying present and taking small steps, Piglet learns to face his fears and enjoy life more fully.

- **Christopher Robin's Wisdom**. Christopher Robin often reminds us to enjoy the present and treasure the time spent with friends. His wisdom encourages us to make the most of every moment and create lasting memories. One of my favorite things he says is referring to Pooh as a "Silly Old Bear." He says this in a playful and accepting way, allowing his friend to move forward in his own way. This tolerance, acceptance, and encouragement create great relationships.

Branding and Influence

Winnie the Pooh and his friends, though fictional, have become influential figures with lessons that go beyond their stories.

- **Pooh's Global Impact**. The lasting popularity of Winnie the Pooh shows the power of being authentic and relatable. Pooh's character, with his simple joys and genuine nature, has influenced many people around the world, teaching us the importance of staying true to ourselves. You will rarely find a culture that doesn't embrace these lessons.

- **Character Branding**. Each character's unique personality and consistent behavior have created strong, recognizable identities. This demonstrates how authenticity can build influence and help us connect with others on a deeper level. Most of us can look within our group of friends and find a character that fits each person. The key point is that we don't have to be exactly alike to form a friendship group.

- **Storytelling**. A.A. Milne's storytelling, filled with humor, warmth, and wisdom, has left a lasting impact. This shows how important storytelling is for sharing values and influencing others. Another interesting fact about Winnie the Pooh is that A.A. Milne had a background as a playwright and poet. He used this experience to tell stories to his son, Christopher Robin Milne, creating wonderful tales with deeper meanings and lessons. Well, done, Mr. A.A. Milne.

Rest and Relaxation

The easygoing pace of life in the Hundred Acre Wood highlights the importance of rest and relaxation.

- **Pooh's Naps**. Pooh's frequent naps and slow lifestyle remind us that rest is vital for our well-being. In a world that often values busyness, Pooh teaches us to prioritize rest and take time to recharge. These naps can also serve as a metaphor. A nap can represent a break from the task at hand. Trust me, they were helpful while writing this book and helped us get through some tough spots. A nice walk through the Hundred Acre Wood was helpful, too.

- **Kanga's Calm**. Kanga's nurturing nature and calm attitude show how important it is to create a peaceful environment for rest and relaxation. Her interactions with Roo highlight the value of a supportive and restful home life. The caring attitude of a loving mother fosters empathy and emotional intelligence, which are essential for navigating life's complexities.

- **Eeyore's Solitude**. Eeyore often finds comfort in being alone, which, despite his sadness, emphasizes the need for quiet moments to reflect and rejuvenate. Many people find Eeyore to be one of the most interesting characters in the group. We can all relate to having a "woe is me" day. The key is to recognize those feelings and work towards making a better day.

Overcoming Challenges and Adversity

The characters' adventures are filled with challenges that teach us resilience and perseverance.

- **Pooh's Determination**. Pooh's relentless pursuit of honey, despite many setbacks, shows his determination. His willingness to keep trying, no matter the difficulties, inspires us to push through tough times. Pooh embodies a Positive Mental Attitude (PMA). He doesn't overthink or dwell on setbacks; he keeps moving forward at his own pace. This reminds me of Albert Einstein's advice to his son Eduard: "Life is like riding a bicycle. To keep your balance, you must keep moving."

- **Piglet's Bravery**. Piglet's change from a timid character to one who faces his fears shows the power of courage and resilience. His journey encourages us to confront our challenges and grow stronger through them. He teaches us to see fear as a tool for recognizing danger. It's admirable how he doesn't let fear take over; instead, it reminds him to be careful when walking into a dark cave.

- **Eeyore's Resilience**. Despite his constant gloom, Eeyore continues to be part of the community and finds ways to cope. His ability to endure sadness reminds us that we can find meaning even in tough times. In past training sessions, I've used the term "negative by nature" to describe how some people see things differently. Eeyore's glass is usually half empty, which is fine because both views can be correct. My seven-year-old son gave me the best answer I've ever heard to the question about whether a glass is half empty or half full. He said, "Dad, it's completely full." When I asked him to explain, he said it's half water and half air, so it's FULL.

Final Reflections

It's important to recognize the deep meaning and lasting relevance of the lessons found in the stories of Winnie the Pooh. These seemingly simple tales are actually rich with wisdom that speaks to the heart of human experience. They offer guidance on how to live a life filled with joy, love, and meaning.

Here are the key takeaways and how they apply to our modern lives.

- **Embracing Simplicity in a Complex World.** In today's fast-paced, technology-driven society, we are often overwhelmed by information, responsibilities, and the constant chase for success. The stories of Winnie the Pooh remind us of the beauty and importance of simplicity. Pooh's happiness with his simple life and his ability to find joy in little things, like a pot of honey or a walk with a friend, teach us to slow down and appreciate the small pleasures in life. Embracing simplicity means clearing out the clutter in our lives, both physically and mentally. It involves focusing on what truly matters: our relationships, our health, and our inner peace. By simplifying our routines and reducing distractions, we can make room for more meaningful experiences and connections.

- **The Power of Authentic Relationships.** The friendships among Pooh, Piglet, Tigger, Eeyore, and the others highlight the importance of real relationships. In a world where social media often creates shallow connections, the deep bonds shared by the characters remind us of the value of genuine, face-to-face interactions. Their friendships are built on mutual respect, understanding, and unconditional support. Investing in authentic relationships means prioritizing quality over quantity. It involves being present, listening actively, and offering support without expecting anything in return. These deep connections provide a sense of belonging and emotional security, which are essential for our well-being.

- **Living in the Present Moment.** One of the most important lessons from Winnie the Pooh is the value of living in the present moment. Pooh's ability to fully engage in whatever he's doing, whether he's enjoying honey, playing with friends, or simply daydreaming, shows the essence of mindfulness. In contrast, our modern lives are often filled with multitasking, worries about the future, and regrets about the past, which keep us from truly experiencing the present. Living in the present means practicing mindfulness in our daily activities. It involves paying attention to our thoughts, feelings, and surroundings without judgment. By being mindful, we can reduce stress, improve our relationships, and find more joy in everyday moments.

- **The Joy of Being Yourself.** The characters in Winnie the Pooh are unapologetically themselves. Pooh is happy with his simplicity, Piglet embraces his small size and bravery, Tigger enjoys his lively spirit, and Eeyore accepts his gloomy nature. Their stories teach us the importance of self-acceptance and being true to ourselves. Being authentic means embracing our strengths and weaknesses, acknowledging our fears, and celebrating what makes us unique. It involves letting go of societal expectations and finding fulfillment in simply being who we are. Authenticity builds self-confidence and helps us form more genuine relationships. The phrase "being comfortable in our own skin," or in Winnie's case, his fur, comes to mind. We may stumble and doubt ourselves, but recognizing this is one of life's greatest lessons. We can return to our strengths and move past challenges. Tomorrow can be as bright as we choose to make it.

- **Overcoming Adversity with Resilience.** The adventures in the Hundred Acre Wood are filled with challenges, yet each character shows amazing resilience. Pooh's determination in his quest for honey, Piglet's courage in facing his fears, and Eeyore's persistence despite his sadness illustrate the power of perseverance. Resilience is about bouncing back from setbacks and seeing challenges as chances to grow. It involves developing a positive mindset, seeking support from others, and holding onto hope even during tough times. By building resilience, we can navigate life's ups and downs with strength and grace.

- **The Importance of Rest and Relaxation.** In a culture that often praises busyness and productivity, the slow pace of life in the Hundred Acre Wood highlights the need for rest and relaxation. Pooh's frequent naps and the characters' easy going lifestyle remind us that rest is essential for our physical and mental health. Prioritizing rest means taking regular breaks, getting enough sleep, and allowing ourselves time to relax and recharge. It involves understanding that rest is not a luxury but an important part of a healthy, balanced life. By valuing rest, we can improve our overall health, boost our creativity, and approach our tasks with fresh energy.

- **Wisdom and the Art of Storytelling.** The timeless wisdom in Winnie the Pooh is shared through the art of storytelling. A.A. Milne's ability to weave deep lessons into simple tales shows how powerful stories are in shaping our beliefs and actions. Stories can connect with us emotionally, making complex ideas easier to understand and remember. Embracing storytelling in our lives means sharing our experiences, values, and lessons with others in engaging and meaningful ways. Whether through writing, speaking, or other creative forms, storytelling can inspire, educate, and help us connect with others on a deeper level.

- **The Enduring Influence of Winnie the Pooh.** The global impact of Winnie the Pooh and his friends highlights the lasting relevance of these stories. They have crossed generations, cultures, and languages, touching the hearts of people worldwide. The characters' ongoing popularity speaks to the universal truths they represent and the strong emotional bonds they create. Winnie the Pooh's influence reminds us of the importance of authenticity, kindness, and simplicity in building a lasting legacy. By embracing these values, we can positively affect the lives of others and create a more compassionate and connected world.

- **Bringing Pooh's Lessons into Our Lives.** As we reflect on the valuable lessons from Winnie the Pooh, the challenge is to integrate these insights into our daily lives. Here are some practical steps to bring Pooh's wisdom into our routines:

  - **Practice Mindfulness.** Take moments throughout the day to pause, breathe, and fully engage with the present. Whether through meditation, mindful eating, or simply enjoying nature, mindfulness can help us find peace and clarity.

  - **Cultivate Authentic Relationships.** Spend time building deep, meaningful connections with family, friends, and your community. Practice active listening, empathy, and support in your interactions. I believe Pooh would agree that we have two ears and one mouth for a reason: listen twice as much as we talk.

- **Embrace Simplicity**. Simplify your surroundings and routines. Focus on what truly matters and let go of unnecessary distractions. Find joy in simple pleasures and experiences.

- **Be True to Yourself**. Embrace your unique qualities and pursue your passions with confidence. Let go of societal pressures and find fulfillment in being your true self.

- **Build Resilience**. Develop a positive mindset and see challenges as chances to grow. Seek support from others and maintain hope during tough times. Don't let pride get in the way; answers can come from the most unexpected places.

- **Prioritize Rest**. Make sure you get enough sleep, take regular breaks, and allow time to relax and recharge. Recognize that rest and a good walk are important for overall well-being.

- **Share Your Stories**. Use the power of storytelling to share your experiences, values, and lessons with others. Inspire and connect through authentic and engaging narratives, which can also help you grow your own thoughts.

The wisdom of Winnie the Pooh and his friends goes beyond the pages of children's books, offering timeless guidance on how to live a rich and meaningful life. As we navigate the challenges of modern life, these stories remind us to focus on the basics: love, friendship, joy, and the simple pleasures of living. By embracing the lessons from the Hundred Acre Wood, we can create a life filled with authenticity, resilience, and deep connections, ultimately finding greater fulfillment and happiness.

The true beauty of the Winnie the Pooh stories lies in the fact that they come from a parent writing tales to share life lessons with his child. It doesn't get much more pure and sincere than that.

www.ingramcontent.com/pod-product-compliance
Lightning Source LLC
Chambersburg PA
CBHW062050080426
42734CB00012B/2597